26 Gorgeous Hikes on the Western Côte d'Azur

Florence Chatzigianis

San Carlos, California
www.azuralive.com

26 Gorgeous Hikes on the Western Côte d'Azur, 1st. Edition.

First printing 2008

ISBN-13: 978-0-9792796-2-1
ISBN-10: 0-9792796-2-3
Library of Congress Control Number: 2007905024

Cover design and maps by Daniel Yeager of Nu-Image Design
Editing by Kathy Kehrli of The Flawless Word
Interior design by Anne Landgraf of Brooklyn BookWorks
Photography by Florence Chatzigianis

Published by AzurAlive, 751 Laurel Street, Suite 808, San Carlos, California 94070; www.azuralive.com

Printed in the United States of America by Sheridan Books

ATTENTION: Quantity discounts are available on bulk purchases of this book for your fundraisers, promotional programs, or as "thank you" gifts to your customers. For information, please contact the AzurAlive book editor by electronic mail at editor@azuralive.com.

DEDICATION

We dedicate this book to all of you who long not only to explore the world, but also to understand it, to leave it unharmed by treading on it as lightly as possible, and to savor and support its local traditions and its natural sites.

ACKNOWLEDGMENTS

This book is about a generous region.

As you are about to discover, or perhaps re-discover, the western Côte d'Azur exudes generosity. Its landscapes vary from soft beaches, shores of ancient red-lava flows, hills covered with parasol pines, marshes where pink flamingos stroll, and islands lush with wild flowers.

Many folks work with passion across these landscapes. They endeavor to protect the land and the traditions that have sustained them. They fervently revive the region's historical sites and help shape its future.

We thank the individuals and organizations who have explored with us another side of the Côte d'Azur: the region's natural side. They generously shared information on the region's geology, flora, fauna, and history. They generously supported and encouraged our efforts to describe the region's trails across its natural treasures.

In particular, we thank:

Bernard Bietta of the Office National des Forêts;
Vincent Blondel of Naturelle Balade;
Hubert Courrier as well as Marieke of the St. Raphaël Office de Tourisme;
Roger Estève of the Conservatoire du Littoral;
Pierre Fernandez;
Marie Garcin Zaiter of the Roquebrune-sur-Argens Office de Tourisme;
Christel Gérardin of the Parc National de Port-Cros;
Denis Huin of the Conservatoire Etudes des Ecosystèmes de Provence (CEEP);
Laurent Jartoux of www.chataigneraie.biz;
Nathalie Leydier of the Service Culturel of the Mayor's Office at La Londe-les-Maures;
Fernando Sandoval of Empreintes Provence;
Jean Sougy of Les Amis de la Presqu'île de Giens;
Bernard Romagnan of the SIVU du Golfe de St. Tropez/Pays des Maures;
Fabien Tambolini

The Office de Tourisme for the towns of Agay, Fréjus, Roquebrune-sur-Argens, Bagnols-en-Forêt, Ste. Maxime, Bormes-les-Mimosas, La Garde-Freinet, Collobrières, Hyères, and its friendly Maison du Tourisme; the local hiking clubs we met on hikes; and the many nature lovers who share with us their passion for the region

The Sentiers de Grande Randonnée, GR®, GR® de pays, and PR® are registered trademarks of the Fédération Française de la Randonnée Pédestre or FFRP.

Col du Bougnon,
Maures Mountains

Giens Peninsula, West side

Cap du Dramont, Estérel

Port-Cros, Hyères Islands

Return from
Pic du Cap Roux, Estérel

Table of Contents

HIKES

The Estérel Mountain Range:
Reach panoramic vistas over the Mediterranean.   10

Around St. Raphaël and Fréjus:
Hike along sights shaped by water.   40

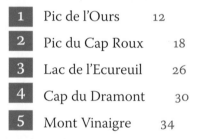

The St. Tropez Peninsula:
Discover the St. Tropez Peninsula's wild side.   64

The Maures Mountain Range:
Explore natural treasures hidden within a sea of forests.   86

Around Hyères:
Walk in the golden glitter of the Provence Azur region.   108

Asides

Giens Peninsula, West side

Aleppo Pine Tree,
Cap du Dramont, Estérel

View from the Dolmen de Gaoutabry

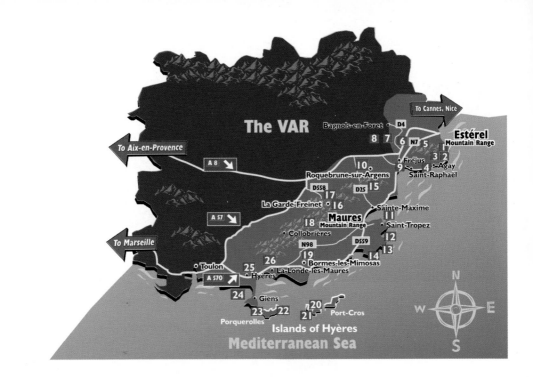

Key to Hike Summaries

Distance:	Round-trip hiking distance.
Time:	Round-trip hiking time at a leisurely pace of three kilometers per hour, adjusted for terrain.
Elevations:	Range of hiking trail's elevation from lowest to highest.
Map:	Name of detailed IGN topographical map relevant to the hike location.
Hiking Profile:	Trail elevation profile. Circles mark the highest and lowest elevations for the hike.

Key to Map Symbols

Car Parking. Hikes on the mainland begin from this point. **P**

Ferryboat drop-off point. Hikes on islands begin from this point

Mountain peak, with elevations.

Fort.

Ruins of fort or castrum.

Castle or tower.

Viewing table that details panorama.

Bridge or ford.

Water cistern used by firefighters against forest fires.

Church or chapel.

Houses or, in the Estérel, forester's lodge.

Tourist Information Office. **i**

Table of Hikes

Coast

Mountains

Lagoon

Gorge

Forest

Grey-leaved Cistus, by Cap du Dramont

Maritime Pines,
by Roquebrune-sur-Argens

Why hike on vacation?

On foot, we no longer belong to the world of tight flight connections, of fast trains that blur the countryside, of rushed highways, of gridlocked streets.

Our hiking pace is whatever we chose it to be. We slow our thoughts to the rhythm of our footsteps. We have time to feel the shade as we stroll under an umbrella pine tree, to smell the fragrant thyme and lavender by the footpath, to notice the crumples on the pink chiffon petals of a cistus flower in spring bloom. We feel the sea breeze on our face. We relax.

To the hiker who knows where to go, the Côte d'Azur is close to paradise. The region may be fast and glitzy, but look beyond its main corridors of attraction, and you find an incredible variety of landscapes: beaches of fine sand, beaches of pebbles, low-lying mountains, chiseled pitons by ancient volcanoes, protected national parks thick with vegetation, plains engorged with colorful flowers, amphibians, and birds of all chants. The region counts a large number of prehistoric sites, some of them well-kept secrets that rarely see a visitor. Many of these sites are accessible only by foot, some also by mountain bike or horseback.

Let's not forget that walking opens our appetite. What better path to a guiltless French meal than a discovery hike through the hills, valleys, and shores of the western Côte d'Azur.

Who are the hikes for?

Anyone with a good general level of fitness can hike comfortably across the paths in this book. You need not be in tip-top athletic shape or follow any stringent training regimen in the months prior to your adventure to complete even the more difficult hikes. If you're in good health, have an appetite for hearty walks, and are eager to soak in the scenery around you, you're all set.

Some of the harder hikes involve uphill stretches that feel almost like climbing, but the more intense climbs are usually short. Of course, you can always rest along the way or pick up the pace to fit your preference.

All of the hikes last from one to four hours. To calculate the time it takes to hike them, we used a leisurely average of three kilometers per hour (1.86 miles per hour) adjusted for uphill and downhill slopes, or difficult terrain.

To keep it simple, the hikes are organized into two levels of challenge: Easy and Medium. On some of the hikes, we suggest easier or longer options. While some subjectivity went in to classifying the hikes (e.g., "How tired did you feel upon completion of this hike?"), we used the following criteria to assign them a level of difficulty:

1. Easy Hike

Easy hikes are either short (two hours or less), mostly flat or with short climbs (no sustained steep climbing), or both. Everyone who is fit enough to walk comfortably for a couple of hours without strain can hop on an easy-ranked trail.

2. Medium Hike

Hikes of medium difficulty include longer stretches of uphill or downhill terrain that requires greater technicality (such as walking over a sloped avalanche of rocks), longer hiking distances, or a combination of these obstacles. Quite a few of the medium-ranked hikes are less than two hours long, but they involve either a healthy climb or, just as challenging, a steep descent.

For junior hikers, we recommend you look through the Table of Hikes to help you gauge what is appropriate for a child's level of endurance and his or

2

her hiking enjoyment. When hiking with kids, we generally prefer hikes on flat and shaded terrain. Here are our favorite hikes with children:

- Cap du Dramont (hike number 4, starting at the Parking du Camp Long for a shorter loop)
- Lac de l'Ecureuil (hike number 3)
- Cap Taillat (hike number 13)
- Porquerolles (hikes number 22 and 23)
- Ancient Millstones (hike number 7)

What are the hiking paths like?

This book focuses on half-day hikes on the western Côte d'Azur, in the Var department of France. Hikes run from island strolls around the Golden Islands off the coast of Hyères, to hikes in the Estérel mountain range. With the exception of a couple of hikes just north of Fréjus, we chose walks south of the A8 highway within an hour's drive from the coast.

All of the hikes take place on marked footpaths, most of them not accessible to cars. The Var counts many such footpaths. More than 1,000 kilometers (621 miles) of marked trails criss-cross the Var. Along the coast, more than 200 kilometers (124 miles) of footpaths meander along the sea on the *Sentier du Littoral* (Coastal Path) in the Var.

The trails in this book cross a variety of land: a national park (the island of Port-Cros), forests managed by the French National Forestry (in the Maures and the Estérel), territories acquired by the Conservatoire du Littoral for protection (see aside on the Conservatory), and communal land. Some paths cross private property, where considerate foot traffic is welcomed along the established paths.

In the Maures and Estérel mountains, dirt paths slice through the elevated flanks. Many are DFCI (D*efense des Forêts contre l'Incendie* or Forest Fire Defense) paths and serve as access roads for not only firefighters, but also hikers and some mountain bikers and horseback riders. Some paths were once sheep-herding tracks. Other ancient paths were used by foresters, wood gatherers, and charcoal makers who traveled the mountains and burned wood for charcoal. Along the coast, long stretches of the Sentier du Littoral hug the coastline. Often called the *Sentier des Douaniers* (Customs Officers' path), the coastline path dates back to the days of Napoleon Bonaparte, when customs officers paced the paths on the lookout for potential enemy ships and smugglers.

While trails abound in the Var department, they represent a few threads among a giant network of footpaths that criss-cross the country. This elaborate national system of footpaths is championed by the Fédération Française de la Randonnée Pédestre, or FFRP, France's long-distance hiking federation and its members.

You will trek on many of these FFRP trails on the *26 Gorgeous Hikes on the Western Côte d'Azur*. The FFRP classifies them into three groups that vary by geographical ambition:

1. Sentier de Promenade et de Randonnée, or PR®

These local trails run in short loops. Often, they offer informative panels along the way that describe cultural or botanical highlights. They're marked in yellow, unless many PR® run close by and cross each other, in which case they can also be red, blue, green, or purple.

2. Sentier de Grande Randonnée de Pays, or GRP®

These are local paths that are meant to highlight interesting local areas. GRPs® are marked with yellow and red paint strips.

3. Sentier de Grande Randonnée, or GR®

These are the giants, the long-distance paths. The GRs® are marked with two strips of paint that form an equals sign, with the top strip in white and the bottom strip in red. In our selection of hikes, you will trek on a slice of some of these far-reaching GRs®:

The GR®51—also called the "Balcony over the Mediterranean," goes east–west for over 500 kilometers (310 miles), following many mountain ridges from the towns of Menton in the east to Marseille in the west. We trot on the GR®51 track in many of our hikes in the Estérel Mountains and around Fréjus and St. Raphaël.

The GR®49—runs for over 100 kilometers (62 miles) from St. Raphaël to the Gorges du Verdon to the north. We hike on a small section of the GR®49 in the Estérel mountain range (Mont Vinaigre hike).

The GR®9—runs from the town of St. Pons-les-Mures by Port Grimaud and St. Tropez, across the Maures and beyond.

The GR®90—meanders inside the Maures mountain range, beginning at Notre-Dame des Anges and going through the towns of Collobrières and Bormes-les-Mimosas.

Some of the FFRP footpaths form the French leg of even larger networks of European multi-country hiking trails.

So while you hike on an off-the-beaten-path trail on the western Côte d'Azur, you're actually hiking on a far-reaching network of tracks that is championed and maintained by many.

When should I go?

If your schedule is flexible, we recommend you visit the Côte d'Azur in May, June, September, or October. These are our favorite hiking months, when the days are usually warm, and the crowds thinner than in the summer.

Summer

In the summertime around the coastal area, temperatures often rise above 30°C at midday to drop in the twenties at night. Generally, temperatures run cooler in the heights of the Maures Mountains and in the wooded areas of the Estérel. We've highlighted those hikes that take place in areas that are more comfortable during dry, sunny days: hikes alongside rivers, by the sea, and in forests.

The Côte d'Azur crowds with visitors, especially between July 15 and August 15 when some businesses in Europe close for *"les grandes vacances"* ("the big break") of the year. Smaller coastal roads gridlock under the strain of extra traffic. Hotels fill up. Restaurants work at a breakneck pace.

Foot traffic increases on coastal paths during the summer, especially on trails close to St. Tropez or on the island of Porquerolles. However, there's enough space for congestion not to be an issue on the footpaths themselves.

The "back country" trails in the Maures and the Estérel mountain ranges rarely become crowded, even during the busiest summer season. An issue with hiking these hills during the summer months is potential closures when fire risks run high. Always check for closures with the local tourism office before heading out on hikes. Each hike provides the telephone numbers of the closest tourism offices.

September and October are often dreamy months for hiking on the Côte d'Azur. Days are cooler than in the summer, but still long, and less crowded. In the Maures mountain range, the leaves of chestnut trees turn yellow, orange, and red in October and November, and towns around the region celebrate their yearly Chestnut Festivals. In the Estérel, the mountains glow in deeper shades of auburn, red, and gold against the background of the sea. The coast breathes easier after the summer crowds have left. During this time of the year, towns and villages return to a natural pace of life.

Note that wild boar hunting season opens during the fall in many of the regional woods. Hunts take place only on specified days of the week. Check with the Tourist Information Office for a current calendar, as these days may vary. We have never found them to be an issue with our hikes, but we still recommend that you wear brighter clothing while trekking during hunting season.

November is traditionally a rainy month on the Côte d'Azur. Rains are usually heavy, but short. It's not unlikely for sheets of rain to pour down one night and for the next day to be dry. The region harbors many variations in rainfall, even within a short radius. The island of Porquerolles, for example, is known to be drier than the coastal towns that face it on the French continent.

While the northern mistral wind visits in autumn and in the spring, it blows punctually on the western side of the Côte d'Azur. It sweeps the skies clear of clouds, making a panoramic crest-line hike enticing after the wind has passed. During those few days when the northern mistral or the eastern wind hurls and the sea churns and torments sailors, sections of the coastal footpaths can turn slippery or even impassable. On especially windy days, it's best to avoid exposed coastal paths.

Winter

In the eighteenth and nineteenth centuries, winter was a fashionable season to vacation in the region, and many well-to-do families migrated here for the mild winter months. In the twentieth century, the trend shifted to summer visits. Today, smaller resort towns turn sleepy during the winter. A few hotels and restaurants even close, especially in January. Some remain closed until April. Spots such as St. Tropez that buzz in the summer quiet down in the winter. If you're looking for bustling resort life, this may not be your season—at least not until winter turns fashionable again. If you enjoy a quieter pace, however, winter is a winner.

Much of the flora that accompanies our hiking paths is evergreen (cork oaks, holm oaks, myrtle, pines, etc.) so the landscape is green and lush in the winter. It is the season when the strawberry trees display, in tandem, white flowers and bright red fruit. Between December and April, depending on the weather, the mimosas bloom in powdery yellow puffs across parts of the Estérel and the Tanneron. In February, towns from St. Raphaël to Bormes-les-Mimosas celebrate the Australian-born essence with Mimosa Festivals.

While temperatures rarely drop much below 0°C on the Côte d'Azur and never stay there for long, weather can be moody in the winter. For hikers with time and patience, walks on clear winter days are especially rewarding.

Spring

Spring on the western Côte d'Azur means the beginning of blooming flowers, balmy weather, a still cool but warming sea, and a trickle of visitors. The weather is uncertain in early spring. Late April through June is usually a delicious set of months for visiting and hiking.

Having said this, the weather on the western Côte d'Azur is playful and enjoys bending the rules. Check the weather forecast—local papers such as *Var Matin* include the week's forecast on the back of each daily edition. Or, take a look at the weather forecasts online with Météo France Weather Forecast (Web site: www.meteofrance.com). Most important for your enjoyment, go with an open mind and a backpack that's prepared in anticipation of the day's conditions.

What should I bring?

You don't have to lug along heavy hiking boots for the hikes covered in this book. To be comfortable and safe, we recommend supportive and broken-into hiking shoes that provide good traction. We don't recommend flip-flops, even for the hikes by the shore. They can break easily and don't provide the traction you need to walk over slippery shoreline rocks. On hot days, stable walking sandals are fine for the shorter coastal walks. For the inland hikes, we prefer closed hiking shoes.

7

Other useful items to bring along:

1. A water bottle—essential for any hike that is longer than one hour. Most of our hikes intentionally take place in nature, away from supply stores and away from drinking water fountains.

2. Sunscreen, sunglasses, and hat—for sunny days.

3. A lightweight hooded windbreaker—for months outside of summer.

4. A pocketknife.

5. A working cell phone—useful in case of emergency.

6. Un pain au chocolat—for added energy. Get one before your hike, warm and fresh, at any boulangerie.

7. A small backpack—to carry all of the above.

If you intend to drift off onto other paths or you like to have a wider picture of the surrounding trail system, get a detailed map. The best maps for hiking in France are those that are supplied by the French Institut Géographique National or IGN (see http://ign.fr). The IGN maps intended for hikers are topographic maps that detail relief with contour lines. In addition to outlining footpaths, rivers, and forests, they provide details such as the location of water cisterns along the way. We find these details of great use when on long-distance hikes. The IGN hiking maps are often referred to as the "Blue Series TOP 25 maps" since they are topographic, blue in cover color, and scaled at 1:25,000. The scaling means that one centimeter on the map translates to 250 meters of terrain.

As with hiking anywhere, it is best to walk with a friend. Although none of our hikes is dangerous, we recommend you let someone (if not a friend or relative, then your hotel, campground, or tourism office) know where you are headed and when you expect to return.

The Var region is well supplied with sporting goods stores, and you can easily find a good pair of shoes, a water bottle, and an IGN map at chain athletic stores such as Décathlon, GO Sports, or Intersport, or at family-run sports shops.

Appendix A lists a number of sporting goods retail stores that are located close to the hiking spots we cover.

A Word about Responsible Hiking

Many of the walks covered in this book take you through sensitive habitats that shelter wildlife, protected plants and flowers, and historical sites. In these delicate natural locations, the presence of human visitors can easily disturb. Most hikers appreciate the delicate balance of life in these habitats and follow these simple steps to tread lightly and minimize their impact on the environment:

1. Stay on the designated trails at all times.

2. Do not pick local flowers or plants, no matter how gorgeous they are.

3. Do not pick up natural objects such as beach-wood or interesting-looking rocks. Leave them for the enjoyment of everyone. Many of these objects play a role in a site's natural balance. For example, beach-wood lying on the beach protects the sand dunes from erosion.

4. Bring a bag and pick up your trash, and why not dispose of the trash others have left behind while you're at it?

5. Keep the noise down so as not to disturb wildlife or fellow hikers. This is all the more important in areas such as Villepey, where bird-watching is popular.

6. Never light a fire on any of the sites covered in this book. Avoid smoking on hikes. Many raging forest fires have started from a cigarette butt being casually flipped to the side of a path. On many of the forested paths, smoking is forbidden.

7. Be courteous. You'll find that many French hikers love to say "Bonjour!" when crossing the path of fellow hikers.

8. Support local nature organizations. We have listed some of them in Appendix B.

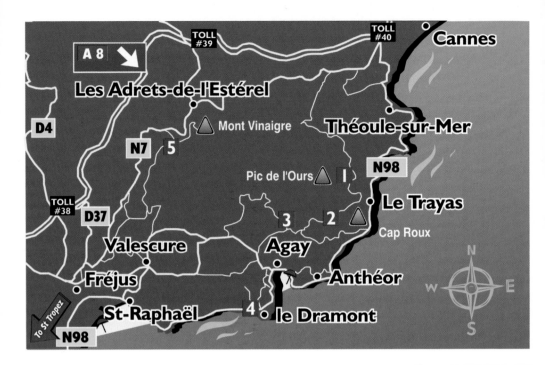

A 8 ↘
TOLL #39
Cannes
TOLL #40
Les Adrets-de-l'Estérel
Mont Vinaigre
Théoule-sur-Mer
D4
N7
5
Pic de l'Ours
N98
TOLL #38
D37
Le Trayas
3
2
Cap Roux
Valescure
Agay
Fréjus
Anthéor
To St Tropez
N98
St-Raphaël
4
le Dramont

N
W   E
S

MASSIF DE L'ESTEREL ▶

The Estérel Mountain Range

Located on the eastern edge of the Var, the mountain range of the Massif de l'Estérel strikes its visitors with contrasts.

The coastline between Cannes and Agay runs deeply carved and the Estérel's jagged peaks of red-lava rocks rise against it as if punched out of the earth. Inland, rounded hills appear gentler, covered in the evergreen foliage of cork oaks, strawberry trees, Mastic trees, and the few holm oaks that forest fires have spared.

The peaks of the Estérel offer panoramic views. From the summits of Cap Roux and Mont Vinaigre, orientation tables detail the surrounding sites: on the coast, the Bays of Cannes, La Napoule, and Agay, and the Golf of Fréjus; in-land, the mountains of the Estérel, the pre-Alpes, the Nice back-country, and the Alps.

At the feet of the Estérel Mountains, beaches between Cannes, Agay, and St. Raphaël fill with summertime beach lovers. In the Estérel, you can hike for hours and see no other life than a rabbit scurrying under ferns, a harmless grass snake crossing the trail, or a Short-toed Eagle (*Circaetus gallicus*) soaring over the hills.

Because of its rugged geology, the Estérel has a tradition of seclusion. In the late fourth century, Saint Honorat sought quiet contemplation in the Estérel and lived as a hermit below the peak of Cap Roux, in the cave now named Grotte Ste. Baume. He later founded a monastic community on the islands of Lérins, whose tradition still lives on today.

A less welcomed visitor to l'Estérel was bandit Gaspard de Besse, a provençal Robin Hood of the eighteenth century who prowled the Malpey (South West of Mont Vinaigre) in search of travelers to rob.

Today, visits are safe. The main danger is that of forest fires. To that end, the park closes on hot, windy days when fire risks run high. The park is otherwise open from 6:00 a.m. to 9:00 p.m.

Check with the St. Raphaël and Agay Tourist Information Offices listed in the specific hikes and in the Appendix for status before entering the Estérel. The tourism offices also organize group walks with the National Forestry (*Office National des Forêts*/ONF) staff.

Dent de l'Ours

1   Pic de l'Ours

Rising almost 500 meters (1,640 feet) above the sea, the rust-colored *Pic de l'Ours* (Bear Peak) mountain of eastern Estérel towers over an expanse of rebellious coastline. As you hike up the mountain, the coastline below, between Cannes and Agay, runs jagged and red and forms tiny creeks like seesaw teeth against the sea. The Corniche de l'Estérel road resembles a river that loops on the green swath of Estérel forest by the coast. To the northeast, the island of Ste. Marguerite and the smaller island of St. Honorat face the Napoule Bay in front of Cannes. As you head down Pic de l'Ours, the hills of the inner Estérel surround you like ripples, an oak forest cools you, and the deeply carved ravine of the Ubac de l'Escale reminds you of the mountain range's tumultuous origins.

We recommend this hike outside of hot days, or in the early part of the day or the late afternoon during warm weather. The hike presents enough of a climb to earn it a "medium" ranking in difficulty. Bring comfortable hiking shoes, plenty of water, and a camera.

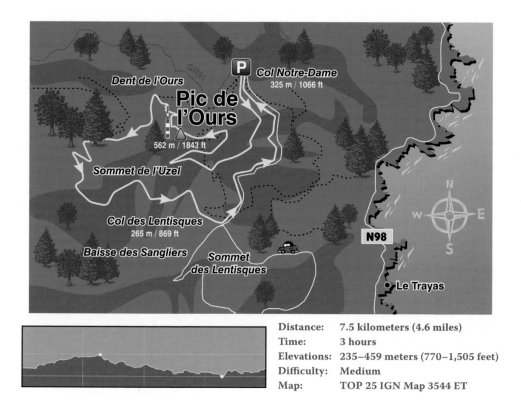

Distance:	**7.5 kilometers (4.6 miles)**
Time:	**3 hours**
Elevations:	**235–459 meters (770–1,505 feet)**
Difficulty:	**Medium**
Map:	**TOP 25 IGN Map 3544 ET**

Getting there:

At the roundabout in Agay by the beach, take the main road (route de Valescure) that heads inland toward Valescure and the Massif de l'Estérel. Turn right after 1.5 kilometers (0.93 mile), after the garage Fiat and the campground "Mas du Rastel," and enter the road with a brown sign: "Massif de l'Estérel." Pass the Maison Forestière de Grata-dis forester's lodge (on your right). At the upcoming fork in the road, take the road that heads down and over a cement bridge. Zigzag up to a T in the road and turn left toward the Pic de l'Ours. At the Col de Lentisque, turn right toward the Pic de l'Ours. You will soon reach the Col de Notre-Dame, where you will park your car.

Hiking:

The journey begins at the parking of Col de Notre-Dame. Take the paved road on the left as you face the antenna atop the Pic de l'Ours.

At the path's entrance, a white-and-red-striped fence blocks forbidden motorized traffic.

As you hike up the gentle slope through pine re-growth, the Mediterranean accompanies you below on your left and the Bear Peak TV relay antenna overhangs you on your right. You continue climbing beyond the hairpin turn in the road, heading toward the antenna at the mountain's peak.

Below the Pic de l'Ours, the coastline twists beyond the village of Le Trayas. It forms lace-like coves by the sea.

You reach the TV relay antenna at the Pic de l'Ours. While the antenna is closed with a green gate and barbed wire, a small path to its right continues

Pic de l'Ours antenna

straight (northwest) under the fence and then heads right and down toward the rock named *Dent de l'Ours* (Bear's Tooth).

In front of the Bear's Tooth rock, you reach a T-intersection with another path.

Shorter Alternative – If you prefer a short hike, turn right here and you will return to the Col de Notre-Dame in fifteen minutes.

To continue the hike, you turn left where you will enjoy an interior view of the Estérel mountain range. Soon, you enter a deep forest of oaks, bushes of cistus, and tree heath.

When the path splits into a tight and barely visible Y, you veer left, following the path's yellow paint marks.

The path opens up and heads left and downward.

At the next intersection, go left. Here, the path is marked in yellow again.

You continue as the path turns left and takes you above the Ravin de l'Ubac de l'Escale ravine. Bushes of Stoechas Lavender border the gently downhill-sloping rocky path.

Checkout Receipt

Library name: M

Current time: 08/03/2017,10:43
Title: Real murders [sound recording]
Call number: HARRIS
Item ID: 33206007204534
Date due: 8/17/2017,23:59

Current time: 08/03/2017,10:43
Title: 26 gorgeous hikes on the western Cote d'Azur : be
Call number: 914.49 CHATZIGIANIS 2008
Item ID: 33206006590032
Date due: 8/17/2017,23:59

Current time: 08/03/2017,10:43
Title: Eyewitness travel France
Call number: 914.4 EYEWITNESS... 2010
Item ID: 33206007545977
Date due: 8/17/2017,23:59

Current time: 08/03/2017,10:43
Title: French Riviera
Call number: 914.49 MICHELIN 2013
Item ID: 33206008672242
Date due: 8/17/2017,23:59

Current time: 08/03/2017,10:43
Title: Fodor's Provence & the French Riviera
Call number: 914.49 FODOR'S... 2011
Item ID: 33206007550449
Date due: 8/17/2017,23:59

Total checkouts for session:5
Total checkouts:8

Renew by phone at:
577-3977
or online at:
www.sanleandrolibrary.org

You reach the Col des Lentisques intersection of paved roads. Here, go left on the road toward the parking lot of the Col Notre-Dame. You may be tempted to snap a few pictures of the Corniche d'Or road that meanders below between red cliffs and the rugged coast and of the railroad that slices straight through it.

After twenty minutes of walking above the chiseled coastline, with the bay of Cannes forming a wide semicircle in the distance, you rejoin your starting point, the Col Notre-Dame.

View from the southeastern side of the Pic de l'Ours

Useful Contacts:

- Agay Tourist Information Office: Phone: +33(0)4 94 82 01 85; E-mail: info@agay.fr; Web site: www.agay.fr
- St. Raphaël Tourist Information Office: Phone: +33(0)4 94 19 52 52; E-mail: information@saint-raphael.com; Web site: www.saint-raphael.com

On our way up to the Pic de l'Ours, Estérel

Also called Spanish Lavender, this fragrant plant blooms in late spring to early summer. Its violet petals, or bracts, form what looks like a silky purple butterfly that sits atop the flower head.

While its tall and famous cousin, the *Lavendula angustifolia*, is cultivated in fields elsewhere in Provence, you will find the Stoechas Lavender growing in the wild in small patches along the footpaths described in this book. It thrives on the acid soils of the Estérel, the Maures, and the Hyères Islands.

2 Pic du Cap Roux

Loop around the peak of the Cap Roux Mountain, hike past the cooling Ste. Baume spring, climb up a rocky path, and discover a grotto tucked in the Ste. Baume rock. A few pots of flowers and candles enlighten the chapel inside the grotto. St. Honoratus is said to have lived in retreat here in the fourth century, before joining the Lérins Islands by Cannes and founding a monastery whose tradition lives on today. Feel free to scribble your thoughts on the guest book by the chapel's entrance.

Back on the footpath, you hike by scree slopes or rubbles of volcanic rock to the top of Cap Roux (454 meters or 1,489 feet). Views of the coast sweep from east to west, from Cannes' Golfe de la Napoule to Cap Camarat on the St. Tropez Peninsula. A viewing table, provided by the Touring Club, details the sites that surround you.

If you have time for only a single hike in the Estérel, take this lively one. It offers a healthy gain in altitude and plenty of gorgeous views. A stretch of the path basks in the sun so avoid hiking it on hot days or at midday when the sun shines brightest. As always, bring plenty of drinking water.

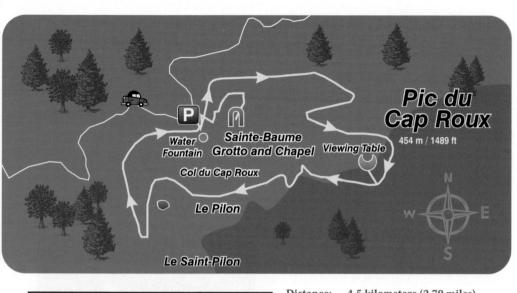

Distance:	4.5 kilometers (2.79 miles)
Time:	1 hour 30 minutes
Elevations:	169–442 meters (554–1,450 feet)
Difficulty:	Medium
Map:	TOP 25 IGN Map 3544 ET

Getting there:

At the roundabout in Agay by the beach, take the main road (route de Valescure) that heads inland toward Valescure and the Massif de l'Estérel. Turn right after 1.5 kilometers (0.93 mile), after the garage Fiat and the campground "Mas du Rastel." Here, enter the road with a brown sign: "Massif de l'Estérel." Pass the Maison Forestière de Gratadis forester's lodge (on your right). At the upcoming fork in the street, take the road that heads down and over a cement bridge. Zigzag up to a T in the road and turn left toward the Pic de l'Ours. As you enter a forested turn in the road, a wooden panel indicates La Sainte Baume. Park 100 meters ahead, where the road widens by a retaining wall.

Hiking:

Your walk to Cap Roux begins with twenty-four steps up a cement stairway. This ascent is followed by a decision at a fork in the path: left for Source de la Sainte Baume, or right for the Pic du Cap Roux?

19

You turn left where the Source de la Sainte Baume water source gurgles in a damp forested corner. Continue left, rising up until you reach another intersection.

Make a sharp right (southeast) at this intersection, hike up, and pass through the fourteenth-century fortified entrance that hangs on the side of the rock. After hiking over a steep ledge (watch your step), you reach the Grotte-Chapelle de La Sainte Baume chapel and grotto, once home to St. Honoratus in the fourth century.

From the grotto, head back down the small path to the main footpath.

At the intersection with the main path, make a right to go around the rocky piton from the north and then east. On your left, notice the Pic de l'Ours mountaintop, with its antenna in red and white stripes. You hike through pine growth and over avalanches of large red lava rocks that crunch under your footsteps.  You head on over the rocky footpath and reach a panel that indicates Plateau d'Anthéor, Source de la Sainte Baume.

 For a panoramic treat, head up to the summit of Cap Roux through the path that faces the panel. An orientation table, courtesy of the Touring Club de France, names what surrounds you: the entire Estérel mountain range, Cannes and its bay, the Bay d'Antibes, the islands of Lérins, the resort towns of Agay and St. Raphaël, and the peninsula of St. Tropez.

You head back down and make a right toward the Saint Pilon. The mountain peak looks like a giant molar tooth that pokes out of the earth.

In front of the Saint Pilon, a sign indicates the way to the Pic du Cap Roux (where you came from) and to the Rocher Saint Barthlemy (not where you are going). Take neither of these options. Rather, follow the path on the right, the one that heads west, down and away from the sea. The path turns around the western side of the Saint Pilon.

You reach a hairpin turn with a sign: Pic du Cap Roux (where you came from) and Plateau d'Anthéor (for a different hike). Take the hairpin turn to the right that heads down. Soon, the jagged Pilon rock appears in the distance with its cave and its avalanche of rocks. You then spot your car below by the road. For a moment, it seems out of place in this haven of nature.

Useful Contacts:

- Agay Tourist Information Office: Phone +33(0)4 94 82 01 85;
  E-mail: info@agay.fr; Web site: www.agay.fr
- St. Raphaël Tourist Information Office: Phone: +33(0)4 94 19 52 52;
  E-mail: information@saint-raphael.com; Web site: www.saint-raphael.com

Cork Oak Tree on the path to the Lac de l'Ecureuil

The Tree

It's easy to spot a cork oak tree with its thick and rubbery bark, its knotted branches, and its dark green leaves spiked at the edges. In the siliceous soils of the Maures and the Estérel, the cork oak tree thrives best on the mountains' sunny southern flanks.

Called *lou suvrier* in the Provençal language, the cork oak tree once reigned over the Maures and the Estérel as a regional golden goose.

Cork, the rubbery bark of the cork oak tree, has long been used by man. In antiquity, cork closed amphorae, lined fishing nets with buoys, and sheltered bees in beehives. In the nineteenth century, cork extraction boomed in the Var region, propelled in part by a parallel boom in the production of glass-bottled wines and Champagne. Cork had all of the required qualities for making fine bottle stoppers: elasticity, lightness, impermeability, and resistance to rot.

In the nineteenth century, towns in the Maures such as La Garde-Freinet bustled as centers of cork extraction. Cork oaks across the region were harvested by lifting the outer layer of the tree's bark. Because the cork grows back on a harvested tree, cork was a renewable material that provided ongoing livelihoods. But the Var, with its exploited land divided into small parcels, struggled to keep up with the cork demand. Meanwhile, cork operations expanded in Portugal's expansive forests of cork oaks and in Spain, Morocco, Algeria, Tunisia, and Italy. Cork production began to dramatically drop off in the Var after World War II. Since the 1960s, alternative and less expensive bottle closures such as plastic stoppers and screw caps have further challenged the local as well as the international cork industry.

Today, few cork oak trees are harvested in the Var. The art of cork harvesting is slowly dissipating. However, cork is resilient. As such, it could one day spring back to an unexpected new life.

The Harvest

Between mid-June and mid-July, when the cork's cells grow fastest, the mature cork oak tree is stripped of parts of its cork layer. Because a newly harvested cork oak tree is vulnerable to heat and fire, harvesters refrain from extracting cork during especially dry weather or when the mistral wind blows wildly. Work begins early in the morning on summer days, when the air still feels cool.

The process of stripping is a manual and delicate one, and harvesters take pride in their

skills. With the help of a special hatchet, the harvester first cuts a crown across the circumference of the tree trunk to mark the top of the bark to extract. The harvester then slices vertically through the tree's thick cork layer and, with the hatchet's beveled wooden handle and a twist of the wrist, lifts the cork away from the trunk. The cork lifts from the trunk as if unglued from it, and as it does so, it snaps with a crisp crackling sound.

Immediately after harvesting, the barren tree trunk takes on a bright orange color that turns darker over time.

During the tree's first harvest, its cork is known as virgin or "male" bark. This initial harvested cork is not of a high enough quality to produce cork bottle stoppers. The tree is left to heal and is

harvested again approximately ten years later. The cork re-growth is called the "female" cork. The finest of this cork re-growth will end up as bottle cork stoppers.

The harvested cork planks are left to dry for about six months and are then cleaned in boiling water before being dried again.

Average-quality cork is ground and used to produce composite cork material. The best-quality cork, the cork with an ideal porosity, is used to make all-natural wine cork stoppers. While cork is used as the raw material for a wide variety of applications such as flooring and insulation

material, bottle stoppers remain the most lucrative outlet for cork today.

Useful Contacts:

- "Eco-Musée du Liège" (Cork Museum of Gonfaron) in the town of Gonfaron. Open 2:00 p.m.to 6:00 p.m. weekdays. Closed Saturdays and Sundays. Phone: +33(0)4 94 78 25 65
- Contact La Garde-Freinet Tourist Office for current offerings in guided tours. E-mail: info@lagardefreinet.com; Phone: +33 (0)4 94 43 67 41; Web site: www.lagardefreinet-tourisme.com

3 Lac de l'Ecureuil

Created by the *Office National des Forêts* (ONF), or the French National Forestry Office, in 1974 to help prevent and fight forest fires, the Lac de l'Ecureuil lake leaks enough water to feed a stream through the ravines of the Mal-Infernet and of the Grenouillet below it. Spurred by the presence of water, life abounds along these two deeply carved ravines.

In the springtime, flowers paint the side of the ravines with bright spots of yellow, purple, and white that glow against the green of sandstones and the red of rhyolite rocks: the deciduous Judas-tree (*Cercis siliquastrum*) explodes with fuchsia-colored flowers; the broom plant splashes a yellow so bright that it appears fluorescent. The narrow-leaved cistus (*Cistus monspeliensis*) shows off its white blossoms alongside the purple flowers of the Stoechas Lavender (*Lavandula stoechas*).

In the summertime, the cool ravines provide relief from the heat while the lake makes for a pleasant picnic destination for the whole family any time of the year.

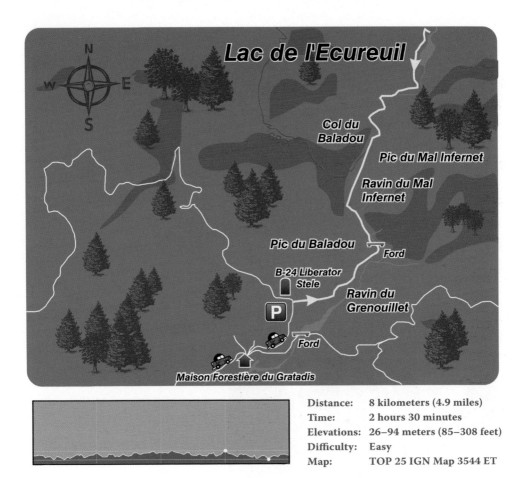

Distance:	8 kilometers (4.9 miles)
Time:	2 hours 30 minutes
Elevations:	26–94 meters (85–308 feet)
Difficulty:	Easy
Map:	TOP 25 IGN Map 3544 ET

Getting there:

At the roundabout in Agay by the beach, take the main road (route de Valescure) that heads inland toward Valescure and the Massif de l'Estérel. Turn right after 1.5 kilometers (0.93 mile), after the garage Fiat and the campground "Mas du Rastel." Here, enter the road with a brown sign: "Massif de l'Estérel." Pass the Maison Forestière de Gratadis forester's lodge (on your right). At the upcoming fork in the road, turn left and go up to the Col de Belle Barbe. Park at the open area 200 meters away.

Note: Behind the parking lot, a granite plaque commemorates the B-24 Liberator bomber of the Fifteenth U.S. Air Force that crashed here on May 25, 1944 during the Allied liberation efforts in World War II.

The wide and sandy hiking path begins beyond the gate and panel marked "Lac de l'Ecureuil." You might share the path with mountain bikers who love the Estérel for its scenery and its network of mountain bike paths.

You stroll above the Ravin du Grenouillet ravine and soon reach a cement ford.

Continue up beyond the ford. A low-lying square post indicates a crossing of paths. Ignore the path to your right and continue straight (north).

You are now hiking inside the Mal-Infernet ravine, hemmed in between the reddish Pic du Mal Infernet and the Col du Baladou Mountains. The words Mal Infernet translate to "evil passage." In the days when bandits and prison escapees hid in the wild Estérel Mountains, some spots such as this one and the Malpey passage by Mont Vinaigre were feared by those who had to travel through them.

You reach the Lac de l'Ecureuil by staying on the main path, which merges with the GR®51 (path of Grande Randonnée marked in red and white stripes) at the Ravin du Mal Infernet gorge. Note the cooler temperature by the gorge.

Enjoy the peaceful and lush scenery all the way to the lake of l'Ecureuil and return through the same path.

Green cork oak foliage over red rhyolite rocks, Estérel

Useful Contacts:

- Agay Tourist Information Office: Phone: +33 (0)4 94 82 01 85;
  E-mail: info@agay.fr; Web site: www.agay.fr
- St. Raphaël Tourist Information Office: Phone: +33(0)4 94 19 52 52;
  E-mail: information@saint-raphael.com; Web site: www.saint-raphael.com

4 Cap Dramont

Perched above the sea and topped with a white, sturdy-looking military signal station, or semaphore, the cape of Cap Dramont appears to protect the multitude of tiny coves and bays that have chiseled their way around it. The waters in the sheltered coves below Cap Dramont shine blue and green like opals.

A well-maintained path loops around the cape. It takes you for a stroll over rocks and tree roots, across a bed of lemony-mint pine needles, and around fiery red sheers that plunge into the sea. Beyond a bend in the path, snug in a crevasse on the red cliff, a bluebird dozes in the sun.

The *Office National des Forêts* (ONF), or the French National Forestry Office, and the French Navy share ownership of Cap Dramont's sixty hectares (150 acres). The cape's semaphore belongs to the French Navy and looks over local marine traffic. Entry to the semaphore is forbidden, but you can hike up to its entrance for a panoramic view of the bay of Agay and of the Estérel Mountains behind it.

The two-hour easy loop and shorter versions around Cap Dramont are popular with families during the summer, and on weekends year round. While a section of the path climbs up and down around cliffs and coves, it is safe if you watch your step and stay on the path.

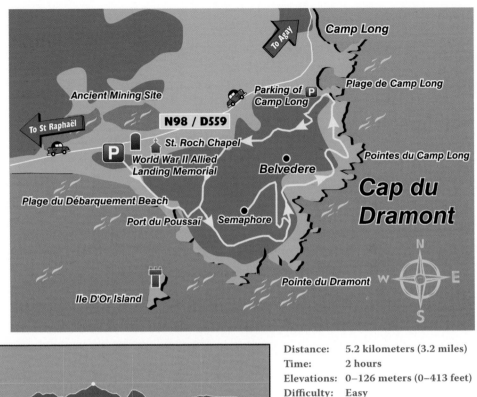

Distance:	5.2 kilometers (3.2 miles)
Time:	2 hours
Elevations:	0–126 meters (0–413 feet)
Difficulty:	Easy
Map:	TOP 25 IGN Map 3544 ET

Getting there:

The entrance to the Plage du Débarquement is three kilometers (1.8 miles) west of Agay's main roundabout, six kilometers (3.7 miles) east of St. Raphaël, on the D559 road that hugs the sea. The entrance is marked with a blue-bordered sign: "Base Nautique du Dramont." On the D559 coming from Agay, pass Camp Long and a string of hotels. When you spot an Avia gas station and the St. Roch Chapel to your left, prepare to turn left into the Plage du Débarquement parking lot a few feet ahead.

On the D559 coming from St. Raphaël, the Plage du Débarquement parking lot is on your right, just after the Hotel Sol e Mar, approximately six kilometers (3.7 miles) from the St. Raphaël Casino.

Begin your hike at the Plage du Débarquement beach, where the U.S. 36th Texas Infantry Division landed on August 15, 1944 as part of the Allied liberation efforts at the end of World War II.

Walk over the gray pebbles on the beach heading east toward the Port du Poussaï. You pass the Mirage Bleu snack bar and then climb up a set of stairs on the left. You then follow the yellow paint signs of the *Sentier du Littoral* (Coastal Path).

After a dozen steps, you turn right toward the sea among a forest of holm oaks (*Quercus ilex*) and strawberry trees (*Arbutus unedo*). There's a little beach on the right with a side of green Esteréllite rocks. These green, sometimes blue, rocks are endemic to the Estérel.

You continue up on the main path, stepping over interweaving rocks and tree roots. You walk on the back side of a group of cliffs. As you do so, you might spot rock-climbers making their way up the sheer side of the escarpment.

When the path merges with a wider one, you turn right. Soon views open up to a string of bays to the south: St. Raphaël, Les Issambres, St. Tropez, and in the distance, Cap Camarat and its lighthouse.

For a short panoramic loop, take the left-veering path that heads up to the semaphore. Although the semaphore is closed to the public, it affords views of the Estérel mountain range to the east. Head back down the same path to turn left back onto the main path.

You now hike up and down around an inlet that is favored by bluebirds.

At the next intersection, turn right to continue heading east on the yellow path close to the sea. At a promontory of red-lava rocks overlooking the sea, take a peek through the pierced crag.

At the next intersection, turn right and head down.

At the next intersection, turn right again. You head closer to the sea after a hairpin turn, and Agay appears in the distance like a maritime lake with the Estérel Mountains behind it.

Walk over a terrace under Aleppo pine trees. There, you might find friends playing *boules* or *pétanque* in the shade of the pines. You reach the Parking du Camp Long.

Note: If you're looking for a snack or refreshment, head down to the Camp Long beach in its sheltered cove below the parking lot. On the beach, the Tiki Plage restaurant is open most of the year, aside from a brief winter closure.

Your return path begins with wooden steps to your left, located above the parking lot, and is marked with a sign and logo for "Belvédère de la Batterie."

Climb up the wooden steps and continue through the wooden right-most path that heads back through the forest then back down to the beach.

Continue by retracing your steps on the beach, on the coastal path through the Port du Poussaï, and back to the Plage du Débarquement.

Useful Contacts:

- Agay Tourist Information Office: E-mail: info@agay.fr; Phone: +33 (0)4 94 82 01 85; Web site: www.agay.fr
- Tiki Plage Bar and Restaurant: Phone: +33 (0)4 94 82 87 88; Web site: www.letiki-plage.fr

5 Mont Vinaigre

A source of debate among those who love the Estérel Mountains, the origins of *Mont Vinaigre*'s name (Mount Vinegar) remain elusive. To some, the smoke tree (*Rhus cotinus*), comfortably established on the southern side of Mont Vinaigre and sometimes locally called Vinaigrier, earned the mountain its name. Others quip that the wine once produced from grapes grown along the Mont Vinaigre inspired the mountain's name. To help close the debate, we sampled local wines from the greater Fréjus region and dismissed the second theory.

Regardless of how its name originated, Mont Vinaigre makes for spectacular hiking.

With its peak at 614 meters (2,014 feet), this ancient volcano dominates the Estérel mountain range. On sunny days, especially after the mistral wind has swept the skies clear, the panorama from the peak of Mont Vinaigre is all-enveloping: from the pre-Alpes to the sea, to St. Raphaël, Fréjus, the St. Tropez Peninsula, and the red rock of Roquebrune-sur-Argens that pops out of the lower Argens Valley.

The length and gentle, steady climb of this hike have earned it a medium difficulty ranking. At the top of Mont Vinaigre, a panoramic (unshaded) platform makes for a great midway resting stop.

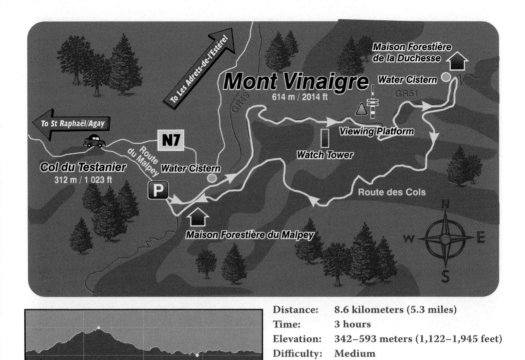

Distance:	8.6 kilometers (5.3 miles)
Time:	3 hours
Elevation:	342–593 meters (1,122–1,945 feet)
Difficulty:	Medium
Map:	TOP 25 IGN Map 3544 ET

Getting there:

From Fréjus or St. Raphaël, take the RN7 road east to the Col du Testanier in l'Estérel. At the col, turn right (coming from Fréjus) onto the Route du Malpey marked H67. Continue onto the Maison Forestière de Malpey forester's lodge and park ahead of it, on the dirt parking lot under the wooden stairs that lead to the GR®49 trail.

Hiking:

You climb the wooden stairs by a wooden sign that reads "Mont Vinaigre, 2.5 km by GR®51," and you begin your hike by eucalyptus and pine trees. One hundred meters up, you reach the GR®51 trail.

You make a right onto the GR®51 trail toward the Mont Vinaigre mountain peak.

After heading down a tad, you reach an intersection with a green water cistern marked FRJ-09. Turn left here.

Fifty meters later, turn right onto the GR®51 trail marked "Mont Vinaigre 1h00." The path is marked in white-over-red paint marks. You hear the distant hum of the cars hurrying on down the RN7 far below, while you walk in peace among cork oaks.

You soon reach a paved road where you turn left (northeast). A short fifty meters later, you head up a little rocky path on your right, where you walk up rubble until the next intersection. You may see the trunks of cork oaks blackened by earlier fires. While fires are a ravaging calamity in the Estérel, most cork oak trees survive them thanks to their thick and fireproof bark.

You head up between the two towers of the Mont Vinaigre then down and right toward an intersection with a paved road. Here, a circular helicopter-landing zone is painted on the pavement.

You continue on the GR®51 paved path up toward the peak of Mont Vinaigre.

At the T-intersection, a panel indicates the direction to "Col de la Cadière." You turn right. The road is soon blocked by beautiful rocky pitons.

Turn left on the steep, rocky path that leads to the panoramic platform of the Mont Vinaigre.

From the Mont Vinaigre platform, you continue down the GR®51 path that turns left and heads down toward the sea. The path is steep here, so watch your step. It soon opens up to more panoramic views that stretch from Cannes to the east, all the way to the St. Tropez Peninsula to the west.

Follow the white-over-red paint marks of the GR®51, and be careful not to veer right onto offshoot paths marked with a white and red X.

The GR®51 descends over Estérel rocks, sliced and diced by nature in straight lines, in cubic blocks, and in wedges. These light volcanic rocks crunch as you step over them. After about forty-five minutes, you reach a light brown water cistern and continue as the path veers to the right down a steep but short section.

At the bottom of the steep section of the path, you reach an intersection. You leave the GR®51 and take the right-most road, the wide Route des Cols, which makes a hairpin turn. Following this turn, you head southwest under the Mont Vinaigre. The Pic de l'Ours appears on your left, with its telltale antenna.

You leave a green water cistern marked FRJ-10 to your left and continue on the now paved Route des Cols.

Soon, you spot a forester's house, the "Maison Forestière de Malpey," tucked at the cusp of the Petit Porfait hill in the distance.

You reach your car, which is parked ahead of the Maison Forestière de Malpey. You have looped around the Mont Vinaigre, in all of its sweetness.

Useful Contacts:

- Agay Tourist Information Office: Phone: +33 (0)4 94 82 01 85; E-mail: info@agay.fr; Web site: www.agay.fr
- St. Raphaël Tourist Information Office: Phone: +33 (0)4 94 19 52 52; E-mail: information@saint-raphael.com; Web site: www.saint-raphael.com

Aside: The Estérellite

Named Estérellite by French geologist Auguste Michel-Lévy, the bluish-gray rock formed some thirty million years ago in a muffled volcanic activity.

While much of the fiery red rocks of l'Estérel formed under outward or extrusive volcanic activity during the Permian geological period 250 million years ago, the younger Estérellite formed under intrusive volcanism, as magma slowly cooled and solidified below ground.

If the rhyolite rocks of the Estérel mountain range, red like glowing embers, dazzled against sea and sky, the more subdued gray Estérellite rocks proved utilitarian.

In Roman times, the Estérellite was extracted from mining sites around current St. Raphaël. It was used to pave roads and monuments and to build cities. Chunks of the Roman Aurelian Way that ran from Rome to Arles exist in Estérellite, as do sections of the Roman city of Forum Julii, now Fréjus.

The mines of Le Dramont extracted the Estérellite rock again in the mid 1850s until 1959, hauling 200–300 tons of rock each day.

Today, the mining site of Le Dramont is a quiet residential area with a few painted homes plopped at the edge of the ancient extraction site. The mine itself has filled with water. The holiday complex of Cap Estérel owns the area, but you can visit the perimeter of the lake.

Once prized by humans as building material, the greenish-gray rocks now appear majestic as sheer walls of silence around the lake.

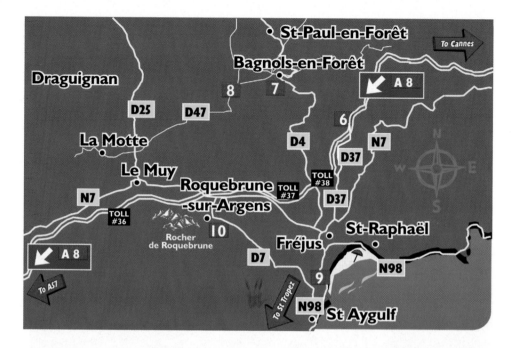

St-Paul-en-Forêt

Bagnols-en-Forêt

To Cannes

Draguignan

A 8

8   7

D25   D47

6

La Motte

D4   N7

Le Muy

D37

Roquebrune   TOLL #37

TOLL #38

N7   -sur-Argens

D37

TOLL #36

10

St-Raphaël

Rocher de Roquebrune

Fréjus

A 8

D7

N98

To A57

9

To St Tropez

N98

St Aygulf

N
W   E
S

Cathedral Cloister, Fréjus

Around St. Raphaël and Fréjus

As everywhere on earth, water plays a critical role in the greater Fréjus area. In the Villepey wetlands, by the delta of the Argens River, sea and fresh water interplay and form shelters for over 200 species of birds and a wide variety of flora. Water helped to carve the deep canyon of the Blavet River by the village of Bagnols-en-Forêt. In 1959, water brought devastation to the region when the Malpasset Dam burst. By the medieval town of Roquebrune-sur-Argens, a eighteenth-century aqueduct bridge runs along the hiking path named "Sentier des 25 ponts" for the water bridge's twenty-five arches.

The hikes described in this chapter take place in environments shaped by water. Enjoy them any time of the year. For the Gorges du Blavet and the Malpasset Dam hikes, avoid days after heavy rains when the terrain may be slippery and the river impassable.

Villepey Lagoons

6 The Malpasset Dam

On December 2, 1959, shortly after 9:00 p.m. while lights still glowed in living rooms, a wall of water forty meters (131 feet) high rushed down the narrow valley of Le Reyan. It wiped out everything on its sea-bound path: roads, railroad tracks, the nearby hamlet of Malpasset, and a swath through the city of Fréjus.

The Malpasset Dam had collapsed, killing over 400 people.

Built in the early 1950s, the arched dam of Malpasset was meant to supply a steady stream of water for irrigation in a region where summers are dry and rains capricious. Under the stress of a vicious downpour of rain that season, and due to fissures in the rock that supported its foundation, the dam failed.

Today, concrete slabs five meters high and three meters wide imprint the valley with a taste of disaster. Rusted iron cables poke out of the rocky debris, twisted in a convulsed mesh.

A walk around the dam remains and the surrounding hills remind visitors of a disaster that deeply affected the region. Many families visit year round on warm weekends.

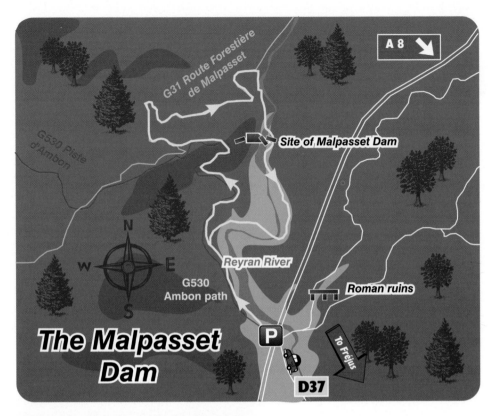

The Malpasset Dam

Distance:	4.1 kilometers (2.5 miles)
Time:	1 hour 30 minutes
Elevations:	35–149 meters (114–488 feet)
Difficulty:	Easy
Map:	TOP 25 IGN Map 3544 ET

Getting there:

From the A8 highway Fréjus *péage*, or toll point (roundabout where D637, D37, and the highway off-ramp join), head north on the D37 road toward Cannes and Malpasset. Immediately after the roundabout, turn left on D37 toward Malpasset. Continue for five kilometers (three miles), cross the river on a cement ford, and continue under the A8 highway overpass to park on the open lot immediately after the highway.

Take the G530 path of "Ambon," crossing the metallic roadblock that is painted in red and white. Leave the path named "Pied de l'ex-barrage 0.6 km" on your right and continue straight up. The wide sandy path reaches a belvedere from where you can spot the gutted dam below. Notice the birch trees in the valley, below what was once the dam's waterline. Be careful not to peek at the dam beyond the safety limits of the site.

Continue on the G530 path until its intersection with the G31 "Route Forestière de Malpasset."

Turn right on the meandering G31. After twenty minutes, you cross an open meadow and reach the Reyran River, where the G31 path ends in a T.

You turn right to follow the Reyran River to the foot of the broken dam. You cross the river and climb up on the path to the other side of the dam. Be careful here as the path is steep and the rocks brittle. You continue another two kilometers (1.2 miles), walking on an eerie path among blocks of cement the size of houses. You then reach the wide G530 path you walked on to begin your hike.

You head left onto the G530 and return to the parking lot.

Useful Contacts:

- Fréjus Tourist Information Office: E—mail: tourisme@frejus.fr; Phone: +33 (0)4 94 51 83 83; Web site: www.frejus.fr

Above and below: Roman Aqueduct, southeast of the Malpasset Dam site

7 Ancient Millstones

Atop a gorgeous bluff, discover the resting site of circular millstones. Destined to crush olives for oil and wheat for flour, the wheel-shaped millstones were painstakingly extracted from this site of hard rhyolite volcanic rock some 200 to 600 years ago. Sometimes pierced at their center, the circular rocks were rolled down the steep path that leads to the peak named the "Col de la Pierre Coucou." The larger rocks weighed over a ton. Rocks that survived the bumpy ride were hauled away in chars or with mules. Those that cracked or showed imperfections were abandoned on the mountain.

The larger millstones on the hill, those that measure between one and 1.60 meters (39.3 to 62.9 inches) in diameter, date from the sixteenth to the nineteenth centuries. Two smaller millstones date back to Gallo-Roman times. Can you find them?

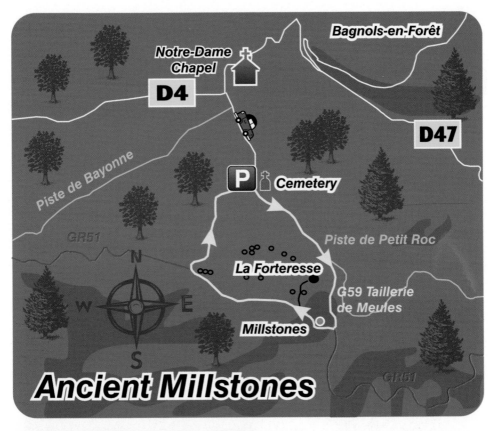

Bagnols-en-Forêt

Notre-Dame Chapel

D4

D47

Piste de Bayonne

GR51

P Cemetery

Piste de Petit Roc

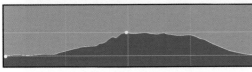

La Forteresse

G59 Taillerie de Meules

N W E S

Millstones

GR51

Ancient Millstones

Distance:	3.3 kilometers (2 miles)
Time:	1 hour 15 minutes
Altitude:	259–415 meters (849–1,361 feet)
Difficulty:	Easy
Map:	TOP 25 IGN Map 3544 ET

Getting there:

Take the D4 road from the A8 highway toward Bagnols-en-Forêt. Do not head up into Bagnols, but pass instead by the hotel restaurant "Au Relais Provençal." There, you turn left on the D47 toward La Motte and Le Muy. Pass the Caveau St. Romain wine cooperative (you can always drop by the winery on your way back). Turn left on the D47 at the next intersection and left again at the Chapelle Notre Dame T-intersection. Drive past the "La Petite Ferme" animal shelter to the cemetery, where you park and lock your car.

From the cemetery, head up on the main road to the large fire path called "Petit Roc." The road climbs steadily and its carved flank exposes a palette of pink, green, and gray shades. To the north, the town of Bagnols-en-Forêt stretches over a forested ridge, like the trail of a shooting star against a dark sky.

At the crossroad, make a right to the G59 path marked "Taillerie de Meules" and head toward the Pierre du Coucou.

At the Col du Coucou road crossing, head right and up on the sharply climbing GR®51 path, which is marked in its traditional white-over-red stripes. The path to the stones is steep but short.

Climb up for about ten to fifteen minutes. Can you spot a millstone or the carving of an extracted stone?

You can return the same way you came, or you can continue on the crest-line GR®51 path, where you turn right by a pile of small rocks and head down a narrow path back to the road and your parking spot.

Useful Contacts:

- Bagnols–en–Forêt Tourist Information Office: Phone: +33 (0)4 94 40 64 68; E–mail: bagnols–en–foret.tourisme@wanadoo.fr; Web site: http://www.ot–bagnols.com/

8 The Blavet Gorges

This hike takes you through a cool, dense forest of oak trees, by the Blavet's rocky riverbed. It passes alongside sheer cliffs. At the base of the cliff, you discover the grotto of Muréron, an opening twenty meters (65 feet) deep that formed when a chunk of rhyolite rock collapsed. Traces of human life dating from 12,000 B.C. were found here. You continue up to the top of the canyon and peer down at the brick-red gorges of the Blavet River. As you make your careful descent back down inside the canyon to the riverbanks, you feel like an eagle diving in from dizzying heights to the coolness of the water.

Hike it outside of the rainy season, when the river swells and becomes difficult to cross.

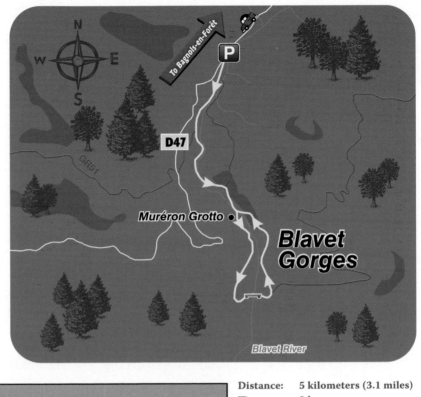

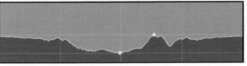

Distance:	5 kilometers (3.1 miles)
Time:	2 hours
Elevations:	95–218 meters (311–715 feet)
Difficulty:	Medium
Map:	TOP 25 IGN Map 3544 ET

Getting there:

Take the D4 road from the A8 highway toward Bagnols-en-Forêt. Do not head up into Bagnols, but pass instead by the hotel restaurant "Au Relais Provençal." There, you turn left on the D47 toward La Motte and Le Muy. Pass the Caveau St. Romain wine cooperative (you can always drop by the winery on your way back). Turn left on D47 at the next intersection and right on D47 at the Chapelle Notre Dame intersection, heading toward Le Muy.

Approximately three kilometers (1.8 miles) after the intersection, a post by the D47 indicates "Gorges du Blavet" and signals the hiking path to the gorges. Park on the left side of the D47, by the trailhead. Lock your car and leave no valuables inside.

Cross the white-and-green-striped car fence and take the path on the right marked "Gorges." The path leads to the GR®51 hiking trail through oak trees, pines, heather, and blackberry bushes.

At the jumble of rocks, turn left to cross the river and walk on its left bank as the path begins to climb. As you do so, you trek among tall pine trees.

At an intersection, take a right and continue on the GR®51 path, which now descends toward the river and mounts of boulders. Notice the "Grotte," or grotto, sign on a tree before the river.

Cross the river here and head up toward the sheer cliff, where you may spot a rock-climber hugging the face of the boulder like a salamander.

The river babbles below as you navigate up through a forest of green oaks, around carved pitons of rock, and reach the top of the gorge. Here, the GR®51 path opens up to a field of Aleppo pine trees and Mastic trees.

The GR®51 joins the wide Piste de la Lieutenante road that you take heading east (left) to a bridge over the Blavet River. Over the bridge, the gorges appear like drapes of velvet in silver, ochre, and salmon.

Cross the bridge and take the narrow path immediately after the bridge on the left—if you reach the "Le Reservoir" fire road, you have gone too far. The path is marked in blue dots of paint on trees and rocks.

After reaching up and around boulders, the blue path dives down toward the Blavet River. Watch your step here as the descent is steep. Follow the blue dots as the path meanders alongside the river in a lush jungle of oak trees, pine trees, mistletoe, and heather. Hear any brown frogs croaking? They sing in these ponds in the spring during mating season.

The GR®51 reaches the blue-dotted path at the "Grotte" junction and leads you back to your car the same way you arrived.

Useful Contacts:

- Bagnols-en-Forêt Tourist Information Office: Phone: +33 (0)4 94 40 64 68; E-mail: bagnols-en-foret.tourisme@wanadoo.fr; Web Site: http://www.ot-bagnols.com/

9 The Villepey Lagoons

Between the beaches of St. Aygulf and the modern port of Fréjus, you make your way around the protected wetlands of Villepey. As you do so, you pass through a myriad of landscapes: sand dunes by the beach, reed fields that shield the inner marshes from the salty sea wind, freshwater ponds, and plots of land cultivated with cereals and pasture.

Life abounds in this natural preserve. Behind a field of reeds that is almost incandescent in the afternoon glow, a black-winged stilt pokes the lakeshore with a beak as long and as thin as a needle. Propped up on beach-wood, a trio of great cormorants stretch their wings to dry in the wind.

Over 220 birds have been spotted in these 260 hectares (642 acres) of protected land, which was acquired by the Conservatoire du Littoral between 1982 and 1997 for conservation.

You loop around the marshes on well-maintained paths, over boardwalks, dirt trails, and bridges. Tuck into the wooden bird-watching hide and you might catch the slow gait of pink flamingos as they walk across the shallow end of the lagoon.

Recommended year round for the entire family, be sure to bring your binoculars.

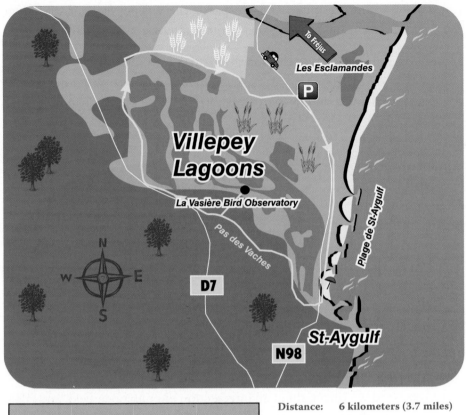

Distance:	6 kilometers (3.7 miles)
Time:	2 hours
Elevations:	0–8 meters (0–26 feet)
Difficulty:	Easy
Map:	TOP 25 IGN Map 3544 ET

Getting there:

Park on the N98 roadside parking by the beach and the Farm of "Les Esclamandes" at the northern entrance to the town of St. Aygulf.

Hiking:

Your walk begins on the beach by sand dunes and palm trees as you head toward St. Aygulf.

You continue to the end of the beach to the N98 overpass bridge. You turn right and walk under the overpass, in front of a hotel/restaurant. You cross over a wooden bridge and onto a sandy path.

You walk by a campground (do not trespass). The Villepey lagoons stretch on your right. You continue past a wooden door and over a boardwalk.

A couple of minutes beyond the boardwalk, you turn right to the "Observatoire de la Vasière" bird observatory. From the wooden bird-watching hide, you might see a lineup of gray herons ashore on an islet in the lagoon.

Rejoin the main path of the Pas des Vaches under parasol pines.

Continue over wooden boardwalks that meander over wetlands, passing by black alders and tamarix (or salt cedar) trees. Next, cross a small pine forest, walking over pine needles and sand.

At each intersection, follow the path marked "Les Esclamandes." Turn right at an intersection after an open field, and right again after crossing a pond.

The path leads you to a paved road, which you follow for a while.

You head right on a dirt path at a right angle from the road. You follow this path around the perimeter of a pasture field, back to the N98 road and to your parking spot.

Useful Contacts:

- Fréjus Tourist Information Office: E-mail: tourisme@frejus.fr; Phone: + 33 (0)4 94 51 83 83; Web site: www.frejus.fr and www.ville-frejus.fr/etangs/ for maps and information on Villepey
- St. Aygulf Tourist Information Office: Phone +33 (0)4 94 81 22 09

It weaves into baskets, knits into fish traps, and turns into fishing rods that bend like bows under the weight of flapping fish. It stands around the perimeter of fields of cereals and protects cultivations from salt-laden winds. It turns into sheds, pan pipes, flutes, salt and pepper shakers, and since ancient times, *"calame (calligraphic plumes)."*

What is it? It's a weed. The "Canne de Provence" (*Arundo donax*), also called Giant Grass, wild cane, or giant cane, grows comfortably in its favorite spots in the Var department of Southeastern France: by the marshlands of Villepey, on the St. Tropez Peninsula, and around Hyères. There, it finds the conditions it loves best: a well-drained soil with water close by and plenty of sunshine. For centuries, folks have molded the tall grass into beautiful and useful artifacts. Today, small slivers of the local giant cane, delicately carved out of the best hand-selected, most-suitable canes, win international acclaim. These precious slivers are reeds that are used by woodwind instruments, such as saxophones and clarinets, and double-reed wind instruments, such as bassoons and oboes.

When placed in the mouthpiece of saxophones and clarinets, they vibrate with the musician's blow and emit musical notes. To many wind-instrument musicians, reeds are fundamental. They shape the timber or color of the musical notes produced.

How are reeds made?
In the Var, the best Arundo donax canes are harvested when they reach about two

years of age. They are culled by hand, de-husked, and either laid out to dry in the sun in conical arrangements or stretched out above fields, where air circulates under them. They are then cured in dry and aerated sheds, where they regain their golden shine. While a

number of local Var growers manufacture their own reeds, many harvest, dry, and cut the carefully inspected canes into tubes for processing by international reed manufacturers such as Rico and others.

Why the Var reeds?

To the poet, the Var reed owes its vibrating talents to the teachings of the local mistral wind. The regional wind, they say, shapes the Arundo donax from its time as a tender green-sprouting grass and guides it to vibrate just right. To others, the mystery of the perfect reed source lies not only with the local winds that bear on the tightness and flexibility of the cane's fibers, but also with the specifics of the soil, the climate, the surrounding hills, the water, and the manual care taken in its harvest.

A reed, as it turns out, is much like a fine wine.

The reed celebrates its own festival each year in May in Hyères at the "Festival de l'Anche." To see this year's Reed Festival calendar, consult the Web site at: http://www.festivaldelanche.com/.

25 Bridges, Roquebrune-sur-Argens

10 Roquebrune-sur-Argens

The rock of Roquebrune-sur-Argens stands majestic above the Argens Valley, like a thick wall scraped on all sides as if carved with a scalpel out of auburn clay. Geologists explain its existence as a "cone of dejection" formed from the erosion of granite rocks from the neighboring Maures Mountains.

To the towns of Roquebrune-sur-Argens and Le Muy, it's an ever-present symbol, a sort of Eiffel Tower of the eastern Var. Called "le rocher" or "le roc" by those who live close to it, it gave Roquebrune-sur-Argens not only its name but also a touch of magic.

The "rocher" accompanies you for a while on this hike along the *Sentiers des 25 Ponts* (Paths of the 25 Bridges). An aqueduct with twenty-five arches runs along the footpath as it did in the eighteenth century when it first brought water to an expanding Roquebrune-sur-Argens.

The hike leaves plenty of energy for a stroll around the town of Roquebrune-sur-Argens. Wander across the town's sinuous roads, under its sixteenth-century arcades and porticoes. Ascend up by the town's cast-iron campanile to the doors of master chocolatier, Monsieur Courreau. The chocolatier concocts bite-sized chocolate "rochers" that will wrap up your adventure in a delectable way.

Distance: 10 kilometers (6.2 miles)
Time: 3 hours 30 minutes
Elevations: 20–278 meters (65–912 feet)
Difficulty: Medium
Map: TOP 25 IGN Map 3544 OT

Getting there:

Take the D7 road to the center of the town of Roquebrune-sur-Argens. Turn left (coming from the sea) at the sign "Cité Millénaire." Pass the Castrum parking (Parking du Castrum) and head right at the roundabout to the cemetery on the southwestern edge of town. You can park by the cemetery, at the Place des Anciens Combattants.

Hiking:

The trail begins behind the Chapel Sainte Anne, in front of the cemetery.

At the trailhead by the chapel, a panel details the paths open ahead. We will hike on the red-marked Sentier des Crêtes. From this point onwards, our path is well marked with streaks of red paint on panels posted at each intersection.

Follow the red markings toward the river "La Petite Maurette." The path turns right into a smaller dirt trail that heads downhill among cork oaks,

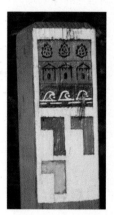 gray-leaved cistus (*Cistus albidus L.*), shrubs of evergreen myrtle (*Myrtus*), Lentisc or Mastic trees (*Pistacia lentiscus*), and the heart-shaped leaves of the ivy-like Sarsaparilla, or Salsepareille *(Smilax aspera L.).*

The trail crosses the small river before heading up into a shaded hill to a four-path crossing. The red-marked road is on the left and soon opens up to the Roquebrune rock on the right. The path leaves the rock behind, while a blue path sprouts on the right. Continue straight to the next intersection where the red path heads right. Continue to follow the red path that is now bordered by cork oaks. It climbs up and soon joins a larger sand road. You may spot a group of goats grazing among pinecones.

Take a left onto the sandy road. Make another left fifty meters later. You climb up to the summit in the company of cork oaks.

Go left and walk down to the next intersection.

At the intersection, go right to the small lake that you walk around to rejoin the larger GR®51 road. You'll notice phone lines where the small path meets the GR®51.

Turn right onto the GR®51 path.

The GR®51 reaches a T that is marked "Bas Petignons" to the left and "Les Campons" to the right.

Make a right here. At the next intersection, turn left. The yellow, red, and blue paths soon regroup as the town of Roquebrune-sur-Argens peeks behind the hill and breaks the silence.

In these terrains of rolling hills, the sun can set early behind the mountains. Hike early to avoid being caught by nightfall.

Useful Contacts:

- Roquebrune-sur-Argens Tourist Information Office: E-mail: tourisme@roquebrunesurargens.fr; Phone: +33 (0)4 94 19 89 89; Web site: www.roquebrune.com/
- Courreau Chocolatier, expert chocolate confectioner, 2 Montée St. Michel, Roquebrune-sur-Argens; Phone: +33 (0)4 94 45 31 56; Open year round. From Monday to Saturday: 8:30 a.m. to 12:30 p.m. and from 3 p.m. to 5 p.m. On Sunday: 8:30 a.m. to 12:30 p.m.
- La Maison du Patrimoine, Impasse Barbacane, Roquebrune-sur-Argens; Phone: +33 (0)4 98 11 36 85; Open year round; July and August, Monday to Sunday from 9:00 a.m. to 12:30 p.m. and from 3:00 p.m. to 6:30 p.m. From September to June, Tuesday to Saturday from 9:00 a.m. to noon and 2:00 p.m. to 6:00 p.m.

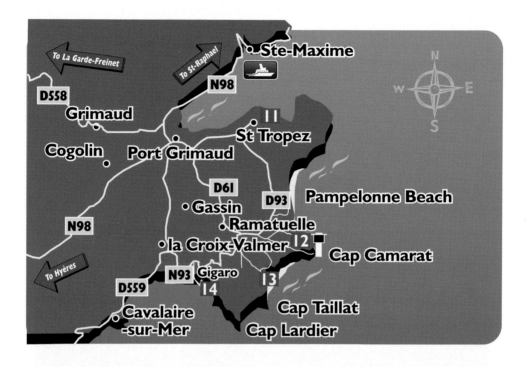

To La Garde-Freinet

To St-Raphael

Ste-Maxime

N98

D558

Grimaud

Cogolin

Port Grimaud

St Tropez

11

D61

Gassin

D93

Pampelonne Beach

N98

Ramatuelle

la Croix-Valmer

12

Cap Camarat

N93

Gigaro

13

D559

14

Cavalaire
-sur-Mer

Cap Taillat

Cap Lardier

N
W   E
S

St. Tropez Peninsula, after the Plage des Salins

The St. Tropez Peninsula

If you think St. Tropez is wild, take a walk around its peninsula.

From St. Tropez, hop on the footpath that was once used by guards to keep watch against enemy ships and walk all the way to the famous beaches of Tahiti and Pampelonne. At Tahiti or Pampelonne, you can kick off your shoes, dip in the Mediterranean, or sip on a refreshment as you reminisce about the wild sides of a multi-faceted St. Tropez Peninsula.

To the south, a trio of capes runs wild. The capes of Camarat, Taillat, and Lardier belong to the Conservatoire National du Littoral, a sort of National Trust for the protection of coastal environments. Created in 1975, the Conservatoire protects unique environmental zones along the French coastline. It does so by acquiring land, restoring its original habitats, and educating the public about their unique ecosystems (see aside for more information).

Around the corner from Plage de Pampelonne beach, the protected kidney vetch plant pokes its bushy gray foliage from cracks in the granite cliffs of Cap Camarat. Hike up to the Camarat Lighthouse, the second highest light in France (the Phare de Vallauris near Cannes is the tallest). Once there, marvel at its focal plane beaming 130 meters (427 feet) above sea level.

Further south, flocks of pelagic birds circle above the slender finger of white sand that hooks Cap Taillat to the continent.

On Cap Lardier, the peninsula's southern-most cape, forests of umbrella pines cover the Vallon de Brouis Valley like a carpet of green mushrooms. The seaside path that climbs around Cap Lardier leads the way to tiny opal-colored inlets and beaches—Plage des Brouis, Plage de Jovat—that are otherwise only accessible by boat.

Cap du Pinet, St. Tropez Peninsula

11 The St. Tropez Peninsula

The hike around the St. Tropez Peninsula begins beyond the lineup of luxury yachts docked at this trendy town's quay. Beyond the cafés that face the yachts, to the sixteenth-century Tour du Portalet, a gun tower looms at the edge of the pier. From there, you walk above the town's maritime cemetery and its marble tombstones. You pass by rocky inlets where waves gurgle and by private villas that share their ocean views. You head up twenty steps to the Cap Saint Pierre promontory. St. Tropez residents once kept watch here for enemy ships and smugglers.

Past the Rabiou headland, you touch the salty brown rocks that are spun and folded like fudge by the open sea. The white sandy beaches of Plage des Salins and Plage de Tahiti await you with beach bars that serve any refreshment or snack you may need before your return trip inland.

This very popular hike offers a variety of scenery over its fifteen kilometers (9 miles). For a shorter loop, return to St. Tropez at Plage des Salins beach and shave an hour from the total hike.

A stripe of yellow paint marks the coastal path. All along the path signs read *Piétons* (pedestrians only) or *Sentier du Littoral* (Coastal Path). The trail shoulders or passes through private properties whose owners appreciate your not trespassing beyond the marked trail.

As usual, bring plenty of water and sunscreen and the optional bathing suit.

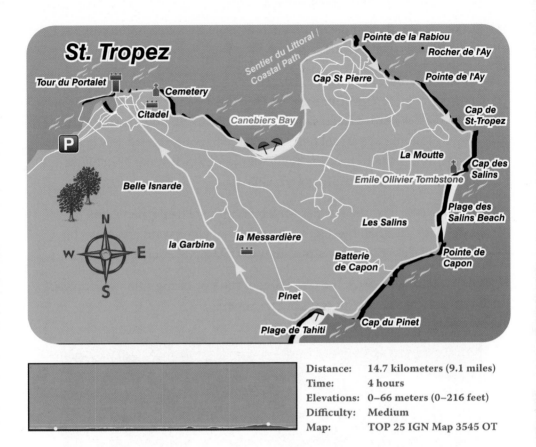

St. Tropez

Tour du Portalet · Cemetery · Citadel · P

Sentier du Littoral / Coastal Path

Canebiers Bay · Cap St Pierre

Pointe de la Rabiou · Rocher de l'Ay · Pointe de l'Ay

Cap de St-Tropez

La Moutte · Cap des Salins

Emile Ollivier Tombstone

Belle Isnarde

Plage des Salins' Beach

Les Salins

N W E S

la Garbine · la Messardière

Batterie de Capon

Pointe de Capon

Pinet

Plage de Tahiti · Cap du Pinet

Distance:	14.7 kilometers (9.1 miles)
Time:	4 hours
Elevations:	0–66 meters (0–216 feet)
Difficulty:	Medium
Map:	TOP 25 IGN Map 3545 OT

Getting there:

In the summer, cars often line up in traffic jams on the roads that lead to St. Tropez. During that busy season, we recommend you catch the bus or arrive in St. Tropez like a star—by boat. From Ste. Maxime, you can catch the ten-minute ferryboat ride over to the St. Tropez pier.

Hiking:

Begin your hike by the pier of St. Tropez, under the Tour du Portalet, where a map details what's ahead—Baie des Canebiers: 2.7 kilometers (1.6 miles); La Moutte: 7.4 kilometers (4.6 miles); Les Salins: 8.5 kilometers (5.2 miles); Plage de Tahiti: 12 kilometers (7.4 miles).

67

Continue around the old port then up away from the coast to the path leading toward the walled Citadel.

Just after the cemetery, a panel indicates "Sentier Littoral" and leads you down to the coastal path. You pass the Plage des Graniers beach, where you hike on a path of hard-packed sand through a strip of bamboos. You then head up to a mount of parasol pines. The large bay ahead is the Bay des Canebiers. You begin to hear the sound of the wind whistling like chimes through the shrouds of the anchored sailboats.

Walk on the beach by the Bay des Canebiers' private nautical club, on the Plage des Tamaris, then head up to the road that climbs and meanders between homes. Pass under the stone door to the Cap St. Pierre.

As you head down toward the Cap Rabiou, you notice the stonewalled villa that mirrors the old fortress walls of St. Tropez.

At the Calanque de la Rabiou, lava rocks look like the milk chocolate that is spun and folded in fudge. The protected beach of Plage de la Moutte soon shows off its white sand. At the Cap des Salins, the granite tombstone of Emile Ollivier (1825–1913, minister under Napoleon III and a great admirer of the region) overlooks the expanse of sea with the inscriptions: "Magna quies in magna spe." This phrase roughly translates from Latin into "There is great peace in great hope."

Beyond the grave marker stretches the white-powdered sand and popular Plage des Salins.

You could head back to St. Tropez from the Plage des Salins by taking the road next to the Leï Salins restaurant. During the summertime, the local SODETAV (Société Départementale de Transports du Var) buses operate back and forth between St. Tropez and various St. Tropez Peninsula beaches, including Plage des Salins and Plage de Tahiti.

Pointe du Capon, St. Tropez Peninsula

Plage de la Moutte, St. Tropez

However, the upcoming Pointe de Capon offers views of a wild wind-swept coastline and the Cap du Pinet affords a cliff-side hike over pine needles. The Plage de Tahiti is wild too, although in a different way. The sand of Tahiti sparkles ahead of you. Beyond it continues the Plage de Pampelonne, a beach that is long in both golden sand and fame.

Kick off your shoes (or everything, clothing is optional here) and cool your feet in the waters by Tahiti Beach. After an energizing sip at one of the beach's bars and restaurants (Tropézina Beach, Millesim Beach, Tahiti, Bora Bora), you can head back to St. Tropez on the Route de Tahiti and Belle Isnarde roads that go through the neighborhoods of Pinet, la Gardine, la Messardière and its hotel castle, and la Belle Isnarde. Doing so, you will reach the center of St. Tropez.

Useful Contacts:

- St. Tropez Tourist Information Office: Phone: +33 (0) 8 92 68 48 28 (calling charges apply); Web site: www.ot-saint-tropez.com/
- Société Départementale de Transports du Var (SODETAV) for local bus services: Web site: www.sodetrav.fr
- Les Bateaux Verts, for ferryboat services between Ste. Maxime and St. Tropez: Phone: +33 (0) 4 94 49 29 39; Web site: www.bateauxverts.com

  A few of the many beach bars and restaurants on the Plage de Pampelonne:
- Leï Salins beach restaurant (Plage des Salins): Phone: +33 (0)4 94 97 04 40; Web site: www.lei-salins.com/
- Bora Bora: Phone: +33 (0)4 94 97 19 75
- Millesim Beach: Phone: +33 (0)4 94 97 20 99
- Tahiti Beach: Phone: +33 (0)4 94 97 18 02; E-mail: tahitibeach@wanadoo.fr; Web site: www.tahiti-beach.com
- Tropézina: Phone: +33 (0)4 94 97 36 78

Aside: Posidonia

Walking along the Sentiers du Littoral coastal path in the Var, you may notice realms of thin, brown leaves piled on the beach. To the eye, they appear as heaps of narrow brown tape.

These are the shed leaves of the underwater *Posidonia oceanica* plant.

The Posidonia forms wide meadows under water, where fish and crustaceans eat, hide, and frolic. The plant prefers to grow where light can reach it, never much deeper than forty meters (131 feet) under water.

Often called "the lungs of the Mediterranean," the Posidonia produces large quantities of oxygen: one square meter (10.7 square feet) produces fourteen liters (3.7 gallons) of oxygen a day, about twice as much as a typical above-water forest.

The expanse of underwater Posidonia softens the surf against the beach and provides a natural barrier against the spread of the bright green and invasive Caulerpa taxifolia alga.

The Posidonia plant regularly sheds its leaves, especially after heavy storms, and the loose strands wash onto shore. On the beaches, the strands pile up into banks of brown leaves and continue their protective role: They shelter the sand beaches and dunes from erosion by the elements.

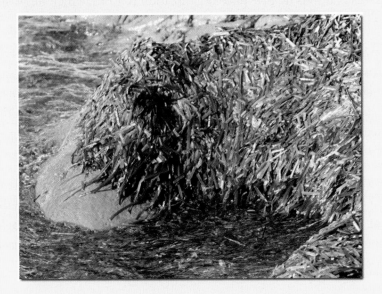

12 Cap Camarat

You'll find Cap Camarat just south of the famous St. Tropez Peninsula's Plage de Pampelonne.

But Cap Camarat has little sand and no beach bars or restaurants. It is a protected site, owned by the Conservatoire du Littoral and managed jointly by the Espaces Naturels de Provence organization (CEEP), which helps support the area's biodiversity, and the commune of Ramatuelle.

In its raw form, Cap Camarat is a block of cream and rusty granite that is cracked and thrust above the sea. Along the *Sentier du Littoral* (Coastguard Path) that climbs up and down around the cape, Camarat displays its rocks in an assortment of shapes: in rectangular pitons with sides so smooth they appear sheared, in thin slices like layers of a wafer, in triangular wedges, and in folds.

This two-hour hike takes you around Cap Camarat from the Plage de Bonne Terrasse. It meanders alongside cliffs of granite then takes you up to the Camarat Lighthouse and down through the inland side of the cape before returning you to the beach. Because of its cliffs, we do not recommend this hike for children.

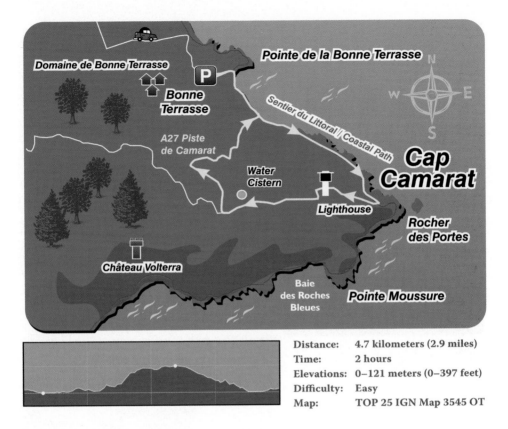

Distance:	**4.7 kilometers (2.9 miles)**
Time:	**2 hours**
Elevations:	**0–121 meters (0–397 feet)**
Difficulty:	**Easy**
Map:	**TOP 25 IGN Map 3545 OT**

Getting there:

From the town of Ramatuelle, follow the signs to "Les Plages," to the beaches of Pampelonne, Camarat, and Bonne Terrasse. At an intersection, turn left toward La Bonne Terrasse. Follow the signs to Baie de la Bonne Terrasse. Park in the lot before the road that leads to the gated community "Domaine de Bonne Terrasse," and head by foot toward the sea.

Hiking:

You take the path of white gravel that leads to the beach "Plage de Bonne Terrasse," where you walk over the crescent of beach heading southeast or right. Hike up on the A27 path, to the Sentier du Littoral coastal path, and pass a tiny house with a broken tile roof.

Jupiter's Beard
(*Anthyllis barba-Jovis*)

Climb over white and caramel granite sheets of rock on the yellow-marked path. Notice the silvery, bushy plants with a straight stance. They're Jupiter's Beard, or Barbes de Jupiter (*Anthyllis barba-Jovis*). These salt-tolerant plants sink their roots through tiny cracks in Camarat's blocks of granite and establish themselves along the salty coastline. In the spring, they blossom with pale yellow flowers.

Continue your hike up the footpath that is carved into the rock, where you pass by tree heath and more Jupiter's Beards. You enter a forest of green oaks that leads to a panoramic view of the Plage de Bonne Terrasse and Pampelonne beaches and, in the distance, of St. Raphaël and the Estérel.

After hiking among thick scrub (*maquis*) vegetation, you reach a rocky path that takes you up to the Camarat Lighthouse. The lighthouse has been closed to the public since early 2006.

Return by heading down the paved road inland toward Ramatuelle and turn right in the well-marked A27 "Piste de Camarat" fire road. Although fire burned parts of the hill in 2006, many cork oaks survived thanks to their thick protective cork. Beyond the hill, a clear day offers views of the Maures, Les Issambres, St. Raphaël, and l'Estérel.

The A27 path takes you back to the coastal path, to the beach de Bonne Terrasse.

Granite cliff by Cap Camarat

Useful Contacts:

- Ramatuelle Tourist Information Office: Phone: +33 (0)4 98 12 64 00;
  Web site: www.ramatuelle-tourisme.com/

North side of Cap Taillat

13 Cap Taillat

Moving west beyond the Plage de l'Escalet beach, a salt-ridden wind whips the sandstone rocks by the coastal path. A plank bridge, blanched like beach-wood and slicked by slapping waves, reaches over a sea cliff. Hikers walk around it. The wind smells of rockfish, crumpled thyme, and curry. On the hillside, a ground cover of Aleppo pine trees (*Pinus halepensis*) and holm oaks (*Quercus ilex*) hugs the ground and leans westward, perfectly sheared. These trees are bonsais, shaped not by a gardener's tools but by the wind, the sea spray, and the sun that reign over this wild peninsula.

Two kilometers (1.2 miles) from the Plage de l'Escalet, the Taillat Cape hangs on to the continent through a finger of sand or isthmus. Not so long ago, unregulated camping settlements covered the beach, until the Conservatoire du Littoral acquired the site in 1987 and restored its thirty-three hectares (eighty-one acres).

Because it is easily accessible and a treat for the senses, Cap Taillat attracts many visitors, especially in July and August. Follow the yellow-marked coastal track from Plage de l'Escalet to Cap Taillat and back for a rewarding short hike.

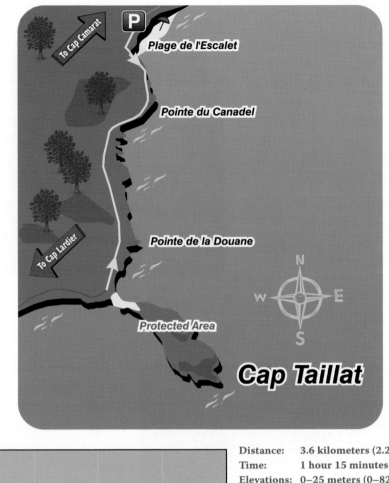

Plage de l'Escalet

To Cap Camarat

Pointe du Canadel

Pointe de la Douane

To Cap Lardier

Protected Area

Cap Taillat

Distance:	3.6 kilometers (2.2 miles)
Time:	1 hour 15 minutes
Elevations:	0–25 meters (0–82 feet)
Difficulty:	Easy
Map:	TOP 25 IGN Map 3545 OT

Getting there:

From St. Tropez, head west on the D98 road, then take the D61 road toward Ramatuelle. Pass the Château Minuty vineyards and at the first roundabout, turn left to the D61 toward "Les Plages." At the next roundabout by Ramatuelle, turn right toward "L'Escalet" and "La Croix-Valmer." From then on, follow the signs for "L'Escalet" where the hike begins. At the Escalet beach, park in the lot shaded by rows of sycamores (also called planes). L'Escalet offers public restrooms and an occasional snack-bar truck during the summer season.

Move west beyond the Plage de l'Escalet beach onto the yellow-marked "Sentier du Littoral," up above the waves. The path runs next to the elegantly curved tentacles of green agaves and passes through a tunnel of strawberry trees (*Arbutus unedo*) and ivy-like *Smilax aspera,* or Salsepareille L., which hangs onto its neighbors with its tiny prickly tentacles.

You walk by large boulders of whitewashed rock, rounded and scrubbed by the wind, the salt, and the pounding surf. To the touch, the rocks feel rugged like coarse sandpaper.

At a T-intersection, turn left and head west toward the cape. Two wooden bridges reach over a small sea cliff that is wet with waves.

You hike up stairs of beach-wood logs, down by Barbary figs cacti (*Opuntia ficus-indica,* also called prickly pears). You walk by Jupiter's Beards (*Anthyllis barba-Jovis*) and by carpets of expansive and invasive Ice Plants (*Carpobrotus edulis and aci-naciformis*) called Griffes de Sorcières in French, meaning Witches' Nails.

The Taillat Cape appears in front of you, hanging onto the path through a thin slice of sand. Wooden palisades (or ganivelles) help retain the sand and encourage the growth of flora on the beach. The vegetation, with its roots running deep into the sand, maintains the placement of the surrounding sand dunes.

When you're ready, turn on your heels and return to l'Escalet through the same path.

South side of Cap Taillat

Useful Contacts:

- Ramatuelle Tourist Information Office: Phone: +33 (0)4 98 12 64 00; Web site: www.ramatuelle-tourisme.com/
- Château Minuty, wine-growing estate in Gassin: Phone: +33 (0)4 94 56 12 09

To Pointe Andati, Cap Lardier

14 Cap Lardier

Of the three protected sibling capes of the St. Tropez Peninsula (Cap Camarat, Cap Taillat, and Cap Lardier), Cap Lardier is the most southern one. On a map, it appears as the thumb on a left hand raising three fingers.

Unlike Cap Taillat, with its thin, fragile finger of sand that dips into the sea, Cap Lardier appears wide and confident, a rounded promontory of forest that broods over the sea. Umbrella pines cover its Vallon des Brouis Valley like a velvet mantle.

On this hike to the western side of Cap Lardier, you hug the coastline to the sound of rumbling surf. You discover coves hidden behind steep cliffs, and a wild cape that points to the islands of Port-Cros and du Levant. You return facing a green carpet of umbrella pine trees.

The hike is strenuous during a short, steep section before the "Pins Blancs" intersection, but otherwise it is comfortable and recommended year round.

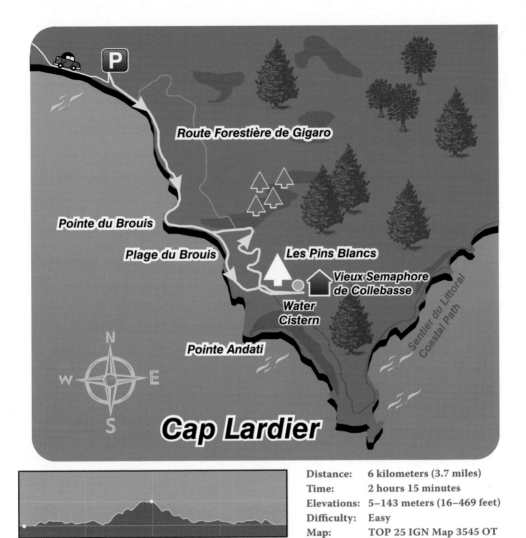

Distance:	6 kilometers (3.7 miles)	
Time:	2 hours 15 minutes	
Elevations:	5–143 meters (16–469 feet)	
Difficulty:	Easy	
Map:	TOP 25 IGN Map 3545 OT	

Getting there:

From the D559, reach the resort town of La Croix-Valmer and follow the road indicated *Gigaro/Cap Lardier*. At the Plage de Gigaro beach, park at the Parking Saint Michel or on the street, if anything is available. Don't forget to purchase and place a parking ticket on your windshield. At the eastern tip of Gigaro, at the beach entrance, the site of the protected Cap Lardier welcomes you with informational signs and restrooms.

The open Sentier du Littoral, here named the Piste des Brugas, begins through a cover of mimosas, holm oaks, narrow-leaved Cistus, and fragrant eucalyptus trees, likely remnants of the area's previous life as a campground.

At the end of the Gigaro beach, the well-maintained path begins to climb. A few umbrella pine trees overlook the cliff. Their exposed roots meander across the path like a jumble of tentacles.

A panel indicates the path to the "Crique de l'Ilot du Crocodile," so named because of the small, bumpy island that pokes its head out of the water. You continue left toward the Plage de Jovat beach, 150 meters (492 feet) ahead.

You navigate up and around a few tiny capes, through dense scrub, or maquis, vegetation. Heading down, the eastern wind carries whiffs of algae and sweet, musty sea salt fragrances. The small Plage de Jovat beach curls up ahead, behind the Pointe du Brouis headland.

In the summertime, when suntan-oiled bodies cover St. Tropez's beaches of Pampelonne and Tahiti, a few escapees wiggle their way to the Plage de Jovat or to the next beach, Plage de Brouis. Feel like a swim?

Toward Jovat Beach, Cap Lardier

As you continue on the Sentier du Littoral, you pass a sign indicating "La Maison du Pêcheur" and continue straight. Up a promontory, you spot Cap

Lardier covered in green. You head closer and umbrella pines appear over the Cap Lardier like mushrooms. By the sea, sheets of white rocks tilt toward the hills.

Sea of umbrella pines on Cap Lardier

You reach Plage des Brouis and continue a few meters on the sand to rejoin the path to Cap Lardier. A sign warns you of an impeding cliff.

The Pointe Andati headland plunges to the sea—you are going to climb away from its sea-diving edge, over a safe but steep path where wooden planks secure your footsteps. You reach the "Les Pins Blancs" (White Pine Trees) promontory slightly out of breath. The spot owes its name to the light gray color of the local Aleppo pine's trunk.

Continue the path to the right and follow directions to the "Vieux Semaphore de Collebasse." After passing a water cistern used to fight forest fires, you turn right to the semaphore, where oak trees, umbrella pines, and the bay of Cavalaire surround you. This area makes for a friendly picnic stop.

You return to Les Pins Blancs through the same route.

From there, you head back to Gigaro, not through the Sentier du Littoral coastal path but through the inland path. The Plage de Gigaro is 2.8 kilometers (1.7 miles) away.

On the wide forest trail of your return, a sea of dark green umbrella pines covers the Vallon des Brouis Valley while the Bay de Cavalaire paints the southern view in a deep blue.

At the next intersection, you head left, back toward the coast. You reach the Plage des Brouis beach and continue on the coastal path going northwest, back to your starting point.

View of the Cavalaire Bay, Cap Lardier

Useful Contacts:

- La Croix Valmer Tourist Office: Phone: +33 (0)4 94 55 12 12; Web site: lacroixvalmer.fr/

Aside: Conservatoire du Littoral

Created in July 1975 in response to the threat of uncontrolled housing developments along the French coastline, the public administrative body of the *Conservatoire du Littoral* (Coastal Protection Agency) acquires ecologically fragile land in France by the coast, lakes, lagoons, and rivers. It then works to restore and protect the land's ecosystem. Once acquired, the land becomes a part of France's national heritage, protected yet open to the public.

As of 2007, the Conservatoire du Littoral owns 100,000 hectares (247,000 acres) of land across France. In the Var département, it currently owns 4,250 hectares of land (10,000 acres). Many of the sites described in this guide belong to the Conservatoire. They include sites within the islands of Hyères, parts of the Giens Peninsula, the three capes on the St. Tropez Peninsula, and the Villepey lagoons, among many others. The agency sports a blue Sea Holly for its emblem. You can spot this blue Sea Holly emblem on informational signs posted within the conservatory-owned sites.

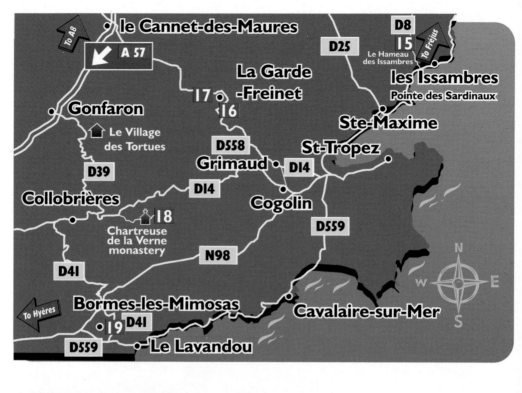

le Cannet-des-Maures

To A8

A 57

D8

15

D25

Le Hameau
des Issambres

To Fréjus

La Garde
-Freinet

les Issambres

Pointe des Sardinaux

17

16

Gonfaron

Le Village
des Tortues

Ste-Maxime

D558

St-Tropez

Grimaud

D14

D39

D14

Collobrières

18

Cogolin

Chartreuse
de la Verne
monastery

D559

N98

D41

To Hyères

Bormes-les-Mimosas

Cavalaire-sur-Mer

19 D41

N

D559

Le Lavandou

W

E

S

View from Les Roches Blanches, Maures Mountains

The Maures Mountain Range

The "Massif des Maures" mountain range spreads for fifty-five kilometers (thirty-four miles) between Hyères to the west and Fréjus to the east. From its northern hilltops, waves of deep green hills ripple down to the St. Tropez Peninsula and to the sea.

The Maures line up in parallel chains of low-lying mountains. The most northerly chain, the chain of La Sauvette, presents the highest peaks: La Sauvette at 779 meters (2,555 feet) and Notre-Dame-des-Anges at 771 meters (2,529 feet).

To the south, the Pradels coastal chain, with its highest point at 528 meters (1,732 feet), rises as a backdrop to the popular coastal towns of Hyères, Le Lavandou, and Cavalaire.

In contrast to the bustling parts of the coast, the northern inland Maures appear mysterious, isolated, and untouched. Neither the TGV train nor highways slice through them, having both chosen to zoom across the flat Argens Valley to the north. Most of the roads that lead to the inland Maures wind through expansive forests of cork oaks, pines, sweet chestnut trees, and bushes of cistus, ferns, and mistletoe.

We especially enjoy the autumn season in the Maures, with the chestnut leaves in flamboyant colors of yellow and gold, the rusty mushroom smells of the forests, and the delectable buzz of the region's chestnut celebrations. The *Festival de la Chataigne* (Chestnut Festival) is held yearly in the small authentic towns of Collobrières and La Garde-Freinet, as well as Gonfaron and other locations.

View from the Col du Bougnon trail, Maures Mountains

15 Col du Bougnon

Aside from feeling almost deserted as compared to the neighboring coast, the peaks of the Maures mountain range open up incredible viewpoints on clear days.

From the top of the Bougnon hill, about nine kilometers (5.6 miles) from the seaside resort town of Ste. Maxime, the dark-green wooded hills of the Maures bounce across the horizon for miles. From the neighboring peak of Cabasse, the bay of St. Raphaël appears to the east like the cusp of a hand that holds the sea. To the south appears the residential seaside town of Les Issambres then the tip of the St. Tropez bay.

Rusty dirt paths slice through the mountain flanks. They serve as access roads not only for firefighters, but also for mountain bikers and hikers.

This 1.5-hour hike among cork oak trees and rocky paths features a steep climb to reach the Col de Cabasse and its panorama.

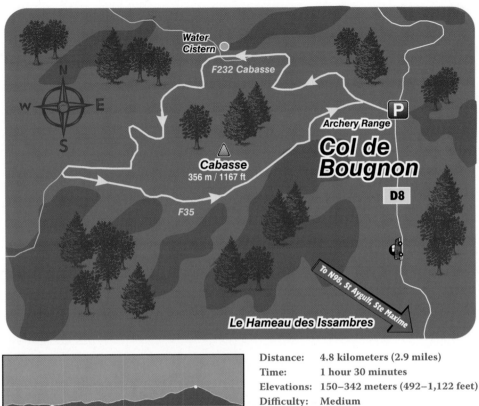

Distance:	4.8 kilometers (2.9 miles)
Time:	1 hour 30 minutes
Elevations:	150–342 meters (492–1,122 feet)
Difficulty:	Medium
Map:	TOP 25 IGN Map 3544 ET

Getting there:

From the N98 seaside road from Ste. Maxime, turn left onto the D8. Head north and follow the sign to "Roquebrune-sur-Argens par le Col de Bougnon." Pass "Le Hameau des Issambres" and reach a street sign on the right-hand side that indicates "Col du Bougnon, Alt 154 m." Opposite the street sign is an archery range with ample parking space. You can safely park there and head for the "Cabasse" fire road beyond the range.

Hike up the fire road labeled F232 "Cabasse." Continue straight on the F232, leaving a footpath marked F35 to your left. The return leg of the hike will bring you back through the F35 fire path.

When you reach a crossing of paths by a green cistern labeled RAG9, continue on the F232 path, the left-most track.

When you reach the F35 track at a hairpin intersection, turn left to hike on the F35. The hill ahead is steep and yours to climb. At the summit, a short path loops around a pillar and affords 360-degree views of the Maures Mountains.

Continue on the steep F35 all the way to the intersection point with the F232 Cabasse path, where you turn right to return to your starting point.

On the path to Col de Cabasse, Maures Mountains

On the path to Cabasse in the Fall, Maures

On the path to Cabasse in the Spring, Maures

Useful Contacts:

- Ste. Maxime Tourist Office: Phone: +33 (0)4 94 55 75 55; Web site: www.ste-maxime.com

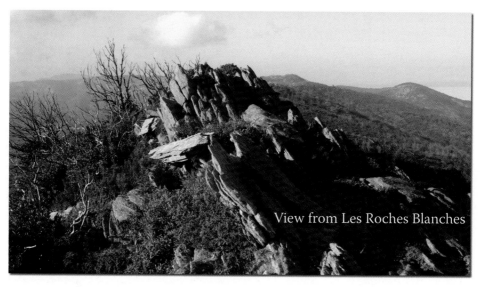

View from Les Roches Blanches

16 La Garde-Freinet: Les Roches Blanches

The charmingly sinuous village of La Garde-Freinet sits at a crossroad of paths. The town was built in the twelfth century in the cusp of a natural corridor that runs east–west through the Maures Mountains from the gulf of St. Tropez and the Mediterranean Sea to the Maures plains.

The village of La Garde-Freinet grew to its current elongated leaf shape as waves of industries thrived and expanded the busy town. In the nineteenth century, cork harvessting boomed in the region, as did silk harvesting and wood coal production.

The hike to the "Roches Blanches," named for the milky-white granite rocks that cover the hill, is especially tasty. You climb through chestnut groves, onto a rocky path, to reach the 637-meter (2,090-feet) peak of Les Roches Blanches. On a clear day, the summit at Les Roches Blanches draws open a panoramic view of the Maures Mountains, the St. Tropez Peninsula, and the Mediterranean Sea. The road that follows the crest-line leads you back to town.

We recommend you start your hike early to enjoy a leisurely stroll through the town of La Garde-Freinet. As usual in the mountains of the Maures and the Estérel, check with the local tourist office for potential path closures when fire risks run high.

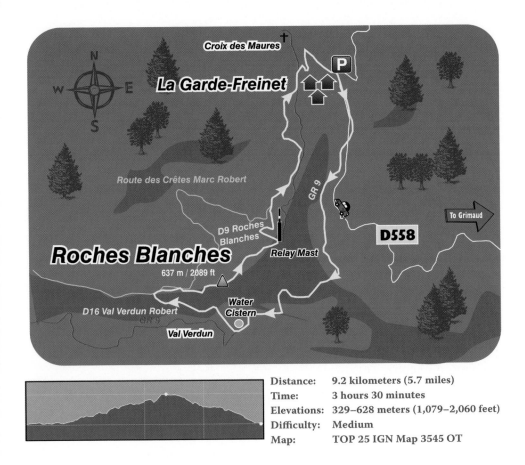

Distance:	**9.2 kilometers (5.7 miles)**
Time:	**3 hours 30 minutes**
Elevations:	**329–628 meters (1,079–2,060 feet)**
Difficulty:	**Medium**
Map:	**TOP 25 IGN Map 3545 OT**

Getting there:

From the coastal road, take the D14 and then the D558 to Grimaud and continue on to La Garde-Freinet. Begin your hike at the Office du Tourisme in the center of La Garde-Freinet.

Hiking:

Walk down the D558 road, heading back toward the town of Grimaud. After the plaza that is occasionally used for playing boules, the sidewalk narrows and a street sign points the way down to Ste. Maxime. About fifty meters (160 feet) away, veer right onto a small road that heads up behind a brown-roofed bus stop.

You've reached the GR®9 path toward Val Verdun, at the Saint Eloi crossing. You climb the paved road in the company of white oaks, olive trees, and villas with majestic views of the Massif des Maures. Along the way, you may spot a few of the GR®9's white-over-red paint marks on telephone or electric poles.

You continue on the GR®9 path as it merges with the D21 "Haut Court" fire path.

After 3.1 kilometers (1.9 miles) on the GR®9, you reach a pair of green water cisterns that are used in the fight against forest fires. Turn right here onto the D16 Val Verdun Robert path of sand and rocks.

After the private residence "Les Roches Blanches," take the path on your left that heads downhill. Soon, you climb again, this time more steeply.

At the T-intersection, you turn right onto the paved road. You have reached the Route des Crêtes.

You briefly leave the paved road a few meters after the intersection and take a dirt path up across an open hill. Here, heath trees display their upswept branches. The short path merges back with the paved Sentier des Crêtes.

From the Sentier des Crêtes, the gentle hills of the Chaine de la Sauvette range spread out all the way to sea. The Chaine de la Sauvette is one of the three main mountain ranges in the Massif des Maures.

Take just ten steps on the Sentier des Crêtes and head straight up the rocky path that climbs toward the panoramic top of the hill. You are going to loop around the hills of the Roches Blanches, thus named for their striking streaks of white quartz.

You might decide to pull out your camera, enticed by the views of the Maures hills bouncing all the way to Grimaud and to the St. Tropez Peninsula. Notice the piles of rocks, or cairns, that are strewn along the way as well as the occasional double yellow lines and the number five painted on rocks.

94

The landscape up Roches Blanches appears lunar. You hike on a belvedere surrounded by flat rocks, some brown, some spotted in peach and gray, some strewn with shiny silver mica deposits. You walk by a flow of white quartz that runs down the hillside like an avalanche of snow.

At the relay aerial mast, turn left onto the D9 Roches Blanches path that leads you down to the Sentier des Crêtes within ten minutes. Turn right on the paved Sentier des Crêtes and continue on the paved road (watch for occasional traffic). Here, you will find yourself amongst glittering mica-encrusted rocks and rusty-colored ones that are stained with ash-green lichen.

As you continue down the paved Route des Crêtes, the Croix des Maures cross appears on your left. Continue down the road as it heads right and descend toward the giggles of the town's schoolyard.

If this invigorating hike has whetted your appetite, you're in luck. La Garde-Freinet is generous in restaurants. Check out the tourism office link below for a list of the town's eateries.

Useful Contacts:

- La Garde-Freinet Tourist Office: E-mail: info@lagardefreinet.com; Phone: +33 (0)4 94 43 67 41; Web site: www.lagardefreinet-tourisme.com

View from the Fort Freinet castrum

17 La Garde-Freinet: Fort Freinet

You climb a short, steep hill behind the village of La Garde-Freinet. You cross a moat that is carved deep into the rock. Step back 800 years in time; you have entered the ruins of the ancient fortified stone settlement of Fort Freinet.

The fortress was built in the twelfth century, in tiered layers, with the lord's home spread across five rooms at the top of the hill. The circular stonewalls below it are believed to be those of an oven. Further down, the vestiges of modest houses huddle together.

From atop the perched fortress, inhabitants could keep an eye on the key passage below that links the Argens Valley across the Maures to the sea. By the end of the thirteenth century, most had moved to the convenience of lower ground and settled in the heart of the current village of La Garde-Freinet. The castrum was destroyed in the sixteenth century.

Legend has long described Fort Freinet as the original stronghold of the Saracens, who poured in from the Mediterranean and occupied the region until the tenth century. Archaeological research conducted in the 1980s showed no conclusive evidence of this, but Fort Freinet may well hide more mysteries yet to unveil.

We recommend a dry day for this hike when winds are light. The schist rocks can be slippery when wet.

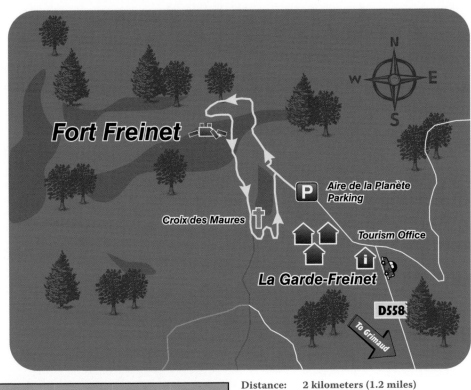

Fort Freinet

Croix des Maures

Aire de la Planète Parking

Tourism Office

La Garde-Freinet

D558

To Grimaud

N
W E
S

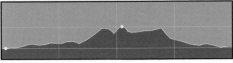

Distance:	2 kilometers (1.2 miles)
Time:	1 hour
Elevations:	325–423 meters (1,066–1,387 feet)
Difficulty:	Medium
Map:	TOP 25 IGN Map 3545 OT

Getting there:

To reach the leaf-shaped village of La Garde-Freinet from the coastal road, take the D14 and then the D558 to Grimaud. Continue on to La Garde-Freinet. From the tourism office in La Garde-Freinet, head up the Rue St. Jacques to the end of the Place Vieille. Turn left and continue to the end of the road, turning right at the hairpin bend. Follow the Rue de la Planète to its parking lot and the wide-open area called "aire de la Planète."

Hiking:

The hiking path begins at the Aire de la Planète, with an informational panel on the Maures, its cork oaks, and its chestnut trees. Continue up the narrow and briefly cemented road.

97

You reach an intersection where another informational panel titled "Balades dans les Maures" describes the surrounding hikes. You continue straight on the path that leads to the castrum.

At the Y-intersection, take the climbing path on your left. Watch out for the path's loose rocks. You soon reach the top of the hill and the moat that is carved around the castrum. Cross the moat and enter the castrum through the steps.

Step down on the southern side of the castrum toward the village and the Croix des Maures cross. Watch your step as the rocks are smooth and slippery. You notice bunches of Stoechas Lavender among the rocks. Continue on the path over gneiss toward the Croix des Maures. After a passage up the next smaller hill, you reach the cross.

You go around the path on the back of the Croix des Maures and reach a T-shaped intersection, with a round-water-tank access on the ground. You take the path on the left that circles around the front side of the cross and head down the rocky, wider path. You land at La Garde-Freinet, at the signpost that began your hike.

View from Fort-Freinet

Fort Freinet castrum, La Garde-Freinet

Fort Freinet castrum on top of hill

Useful Contacts:

- La Garde-Freinet Tourist Office: E-mail: info@lagardefreinet.com; Phone: +33 (0)4 94 43 67 41; Web site: www.lagardefreinet-tourisme.com

18 Chartreuse de la Verne

It floats over waves of dark hills in the Maures Mountains, a long, thin, tawny-brown ship with arcades for portholes, rows of roofed cubic cells for living quarters, and the pointed bell tower of its church for a pilothouse. Behind a forest of chestnut and holm oaks, the La Verne Chartreuse glows in the browns of its local schist rocks and the greens of its serpentine doorframes and vaults.

The history of this Carthusian monastery is one of turbulence and tenacity. Founded in 1170 over the site of an old presbytery, the La Verne Charterhouse endured ravaging fires, assaults, and pillages. After each wave of destruction, it supporters picked up rubbles, cleared ashes and loss, and rebuilt. In 1790, after the French Revolution, the Charterhouse's goods were sequestered and the monks were forced to abandon the monastery.

Classified as an historical monument in 1921, it was "adopted" in 1968 by a group of dedicated friends ("L'Association des Amis de la Verne") and restored. Since 1983, sisters from the religious order of Bethlehem have lived in the monastery.

Parts of the monastery are open to the public for quiet visits every day 11:00 a.m. to 5:00 p.m., except Tuesdays and during the month of January, when the building is closed.

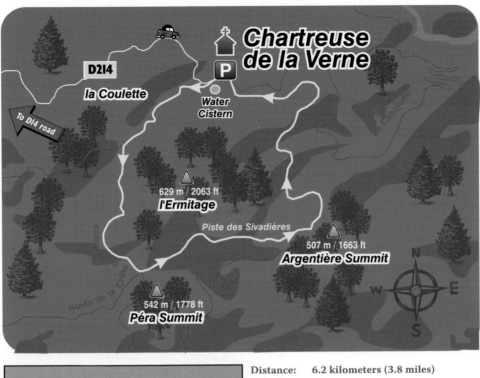

Chartreuse de la Verne

D214

la Coulette

To D14 road

Water Cistern

629 m / 2063 ft
l'Ermitage

Piste des Sivadières

507 m / 1663 ft
Argentière Summit

542 m / 1778 ft
Péra Summit

Distance:	6.2 kilometers (3.8 miles)
Time:	2 hours 15 minutes
Elevations:	401–546 meters (1,315–1,791 feet)
Difficulty:	Easy
Map:	TOP 25 IGN Map 3545 OT

Getting there:

From Grimaud, take the D14 road toward La Garde-Freinet. Veer left on its narrow, winding path toward Collobrières. Head left onto D214 to reach the Le Monastère de la Verne. Park in the parking lot in front of the monastery.

Hiking:

You begin this easy hike by walking a few steps back onto the D214 road to a rusty old water cistern on your left, just before the parking lot. A path is marked "Plateau Lambert, 8.9 km." Although you won't be hiking all the way to the plateau, you head up this little path, walking among holm oaks and sweet chestnut trees.

After one kilometer (0.6 mile), you reach La Coulette. Continue straight on the somewhat-paved road marked "Retenue d'Eau de Lambert" to the top of the Péra Hill.

At the wide-open space of the Sommet du Péra, turn left onto the B17 fire road called Sivadières.

On the Sivadières path, you reach the Argentière summit, where a number of paths cross the "B18 Le Noyer" fire road on the right and the "B36 Les Campaux." You continue straight on the Maures path or "Chemin des Maures."

After fifteen minutes, you find yourself at the "La Verne" intersection, where you head down to your right and soon spot the monastery ahead. This section of your hike leads you down through a grove of giant, sweet chestnut trees, back to the eastern edge of the Chartreuse building.

Useful Contacts:

- Monastère de la Verne: Phone: +33 (0)4 94 43 48 28
- Collobrières Tourist Information Office: E–mail: contact@collobrieres–tourisme.com; Phone: +33 (0)4 94 48 08 00; Web site: www.collobrieres–tourisme.com

At the yearly
Chestnut Festival,
Collobrières,
Maures Mountains

103

Oratory on the path up to Chapel Notre-Dame de Constance, Bormes-les-Mimosas

19 Bormes-les-Mimosas

Covered in yellow mimosas from late January to March and in bright pink bougainvilleas from June, the old town of Bormes-les-Mimosas bursts with colors like a firework. Some ninety varieties of mimosas flourish here, each doused in scents of vanilla and sweet pineapple and flush with powdery yellow balls like little rounded honey drops.

The town's roads climb around *la rue Rompi Cuou* (the break-neck road). They rest by the eighteenth-century St. Trophyme church, where under a big yellow tree a bench faces a bougainvillea. Neat and well-restored, the roads take cover under stone passageways, or "cuberts."

The round-trip hike through the streets of Bormes-les-Mimosas to the Chapel Notre-Dame de Constance isn't a "rompi cuou" walk, but it climbs to reach 324 meters (1,062 feet). At the top of the hill by the chapel, an orientation table names the blue, green, and golden sites that surround and dazzle you from the mountains of the Maures to the Golden Islands of Hyères.

We highly recommend this panoramic hike.

Distance:	3.3 kilometers (2 miles)
Time:	1 hour 15 minutes
Elevations:	153–324 meters (501–1,062 feet)
Difficulty:	Easy
Map:	TOP 25 IGN Map 3446 ET

Getting there:

Take the N98 road heading west from St. Tropez or east from Hyères. Then take the D559 (from Hyères) or the D41 (from St. Tropez) to reach the well-indicated Bormes-les-Mimosas. Park your car in the large parking garage next to the St.-François de Paule Chapel.

Hiking:

Head west toward the center of town. Pass the tourism office at Place Gambetta. Head up the Rue du Dr. Bérenguier road and follow the sign for Château Notre-Dame de Constance.

Fifty meters (160 feet) ahead, at the Avenue des Lauriers Roses, veer left. All around, giant agaves spread their water-filled leaves.

A few steps later, turn right on the paved alley named "Traverse du Chateau" that whisks you up to the thirteenth- and fourteenth-century castle of the Lords of Fos (Château des Seigneurs de Fos). The castle is private and entry is forbidden. The adjoining small park offers a bench in the shade of parasol pines.

You turn right on the "Circuit Pédestre" GR®90 road and head up. You will be following the GR®90 with its white-over-red paint marks all the way to the chapel.

The GR®90 briefly enters the A640 "Fontane" path and turns right at the "Notre-Dame de Constance" sign, by a mount of rocks. You climb on this path of sparkling mica rocks with specks of white quartz. Oratories border the path. At the top of the hill, a few cypress trees, sharpened like pencils, point to the sky.

The way up to Notre-Dame de Constance is short, but steep

Observation table by Notre-Dame de Constance

The Chapel of Notre-Dame de Constance appears and you marvel at the views around the observation table: the seaside resort town of Le Lavandou, the islands of Hyères, and the hills of the Maures. You walk down the other side of the hill on a wide, sandy path.

As the GR®90 continues straight on a path that narrows, you turn left onto a wider path that is bordered with cork oaks. As you do so, you notice the red rocks planted on the hillside like megaliths.

When you reach a green water cistern labeled BLM 09, you veer left onto the A640 Fontone fire road. To your sides, caramel-brown rocks stand upright.

In the distance, you spot the Hyères islands of l'Ile du Levant (larger easternmost island), l'Ile de Port Cros (smaller bumpy island), and l'Ile de Porquerolles. The castle of the Lords of Fos reappears. You've returned home.

Useful Contacts:

- Bormes–les–Mimosas Tourist Information Office: Phone: +33 (0)4 94 01 38 38; E–mail: mail@bormeslesmimosas.com; Web site: www.bormeslesmimosas.com

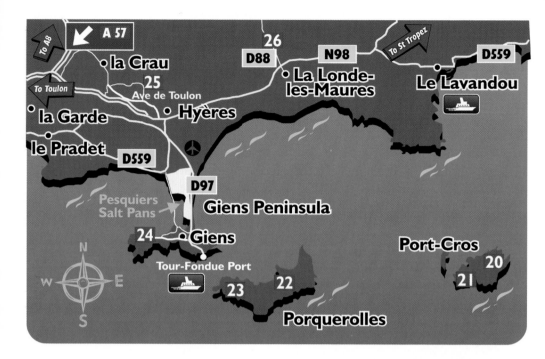

Porquerolles, Plage de la Courtade

Around Hyères

The city of Hyères deserves a long stroll along its staple palm trees that sway in the breeze. Its stately villas, its plush gardens, and its flowered streets have earned the city its status of *ville fleurie* (flowered city). Hotels of marble and sunlight such as the Grand Hotel, the Hotel des Palmiers, and the Park Hotel remind visitors of the town's status as a grand winter resort during the nineteenth century. Today, Hyères appears lively and balanced, a vibrant town where tourism plays one role among many.

Legend has it that the three main islands off the coast of Hyères (Ile du Levant, Ile de Port-Cros, and Ile de Porquerolles) that line up east to west and almost touch the Giens Peninsula are three sisters. When thieves tried to whisk the girls away, the girls' brother turned his sisters into rocks to seal their fate away from the kidnappers.

Also named Golden Islands (*Iles d'Or*), no doubt for the way the sun paints them at dawn and dusk, the islands were once attached to the continent and were part of the Maures mountain chain. They share the warm brown and beige colors of mica shale rocks with the Maures Mountains.

Many visitors have passed through the islands: the Ligurians; the Greeks, who called the string of islands the *Stochaedes* (in a row) for their alignment; the Romans; and the Saracens, who used the islands as bases for their expeditions inland. In the sixteenth century, after waves of pirates had repeatedly pillaged the islands, French King Francois I ordered the construction of forts as did French Cardinal Richelieu in the seventeenth century. Understanding the island's strategic military location, Napoleon solidified a number of the forts, which still stand today.

The Iles d'Hyères now attract visitors who seek a reprieve from the buzz of highways and the clinging shuffle of hurried heals on pavements. There are no cars on the islands, other than a handful of service vehicles that are authorized for local use.

On Porquerolles, mountain bikes zip by the island's many well-maintained paths. On Port-Cros, a national park in its entirety, neither cars nor bikes are allowed, making the protected island a hiker's paradise.

We won't hike on the Ile du Levant as most of the island is owned by the French Navy and is off limits to visitors outside of the naturalist village of Héliopolis.

Facing the islands of Hyères and almost an island itself, the Giens Peninsula hangs on to the continent through two thin sandbars. Land of French poet Saint John Perse, the Giens Peninsula harbors a western coastline that is wild with sheer cliffs and thick forests of maquis scrub.

Fifteen minutes inland from Hyères, the Mont Fenouillet Mountain overlooks Hyères, its coastline, the double isthmus of the Giens Peninsula, the Golden Islands, the mountains of the Maurettes and the Maures to the east, and Toulon's backdrop of chalk-white limestone hills to the west.

Useful Contacts:

The most frequent ferryboats bound for the islands of Hyères take off from the Port St. Pierre of Hyères (for Port-Cros with a one-hour crossing and Le Levant with a one-hour-and-thirty-minute crossing) and from La Tour Fondue on the Giens Peninsula for Porquerolles (twenty-minute crossing).

During the busier summer season, many other ports of the Var serve the Iles d'Or, including Toulon, La Londe-les-Maures, Le Lavandou, Cavalaire, St. Tropez, and St. Raphaël.

- TLV Transports Littoral Varois: Phone: +33 (0)4 94 58 21 81; E-mail: infos@tlv-tvm.com; Web site: www.tlv-tvm.com for ferryboat access from Hyères and the Giens Peninsula

- Vedettes des Iles d'Or: Web site: www.vedettesilesdor.fr for ferryboat access from La Croix-Valmer, Le Lavandou, Cavalaire, and La Londe-les-Maures

View from the Sentier des Plantes, Port-Cros

From the Sentier des Crêtes, Port-Cros

By the Rocher du Rascas, Port-Cros

20 Port-Cros: Sentier des Plantes

On Port-Cros' only port, behind the rocky Bagaud islet, the ferryboat drops off a handful of visitors, all strapped with backpacks and hiking boots. Under the shade of palm trees, a couple of restaurants line up to face the little port's three floating decks.

Hillier and more rugged than its big sister Porquerolles, the Ile d'Or island of Port-Cros draws to its shores those who long for a slice of raw nature. You come on this conch-shell-shaped island to escape, to live marooned like a Robinson Crusoe among a lush vegetation of rock samphire (*Crithmum maritimum*), silvery shrubs of Jupiter's Beards (*Anthyllis barba-Jovis*), and bright, tender green Mediterranean Spurge (*Euphorbe characias*). You hike above cliffs of brown schist rocks that drop into the sea. As the paths curb, the cliffs yield to a few sheltered coves and the island's main beaches: Plage du Sud, Plage de Port Cros, Plage de la Palud, and Plage de Port-Man. In the heart of the island, forests of green oaks cover the humid and mysterious inside vallons.

Prepare for your adventure on gorgeous Port-Cros with plenty of water and picnic supplies. You will find no supply stores or drinking-water sources outside the shops by the port. Also, bring a mask, snorkel, and fins for an underwater exploration.

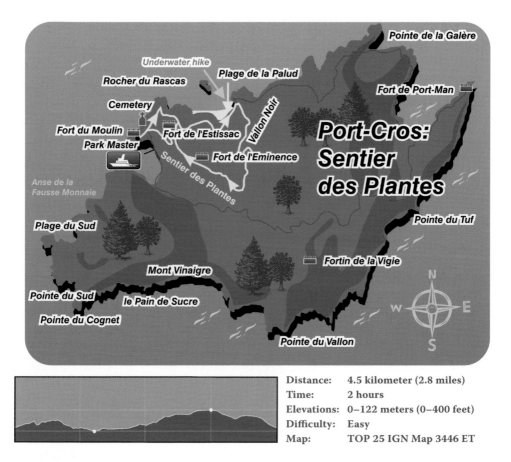

Distance:	4.5 kilometer (2.8 miles)
Time:	2 hours
Elevations:	0–122 meters (0–400 feet)
Difficulty:	Easy
Map:	TOP 25 IGN Map 3446 ET

For information on ferryboat access to Port-Cros, see chapter introduction.

Hiking:

Begin your hike by the port, at the national park's capitainerie. You will find information on the island and plastic aqua-guides to help you identify your snorkeling discoveries if you opt to include the underwater part of the hike.

You then head up to the Fort du Moulin, which overlooks the port. (Access to the sixteenth-century fort is closed.)

Rejoin the *Sentier des Plantes* (Botanical Footpath) at the top of the stone stairs. The Plage de la Palud, an ideal spot to picnic and the underwater trail's location, awaits you about thirty minutes out. You walk by the island's tiny cemetery, by its salt-sweating tamarix trees, by its Aleppo pine trees, and by its bushes of rosemary. You soon spot the *Rocher du Rascas (*Rascas Rock) out to sea.

Through a gorgeous walk around the cape, you head down to the sheltered bay of la Palud. Its bright circles of turquoise tantalize the eye as seagulls circle above the Rascas Rock. In the summer, you can trade hiking shoes for fins, plunge into the bay, and marvel at the variety of fish along the marked underwater trail (see Aside for details).

When the time comes to head back, reach the northeast side of the bay of la Palud and take the path indicating "Village par Vallon Noir."

Down to la Palud, Port-Cros

Following a thick and dark forest of oak trees, turn right to continue your return to the village, now forty-five minutes away.

At the green water cistern, turn right toward the village. You climb gently on the comfortable path by the next green cistern, where you head right again, following the signs for the village. On the side of the road, notice the schist rocks that are thinly layered like a mille-feuille pastry.

Take the next brief detour up to the Fort de l'Eminence, which was built by Richelieu in the seventeenth century and is now open to the public during the summer.

Fort de l'Eminence, Port-Cros

The fort offers viewpoints of the semicircle bay of la Palud, all the way to the tip of the island.

Return to the main path and continue your way down. At the next intersection, head down the smaller path toward "le village" on the right, and continue on straight down to the port.

From the pier, Port-Cros

Plage de la Palud, Photo © Ch. Gérardin, PN Port-Cros

The beach of la Palud on Port-Cros is the perfect spot to take off hiking boots, fit fins on feet, and dip in the bay's translucent waters. Between the beach and the rock of Rascas that shelters the bay of la Palud, the National Park of Port-Cros has set up an underwater discovery trail.

The triangular area is restricted to swimmers and divers only. It is set up with a string of yellow buoys that mark the underwater trail. Below each buoy hangs a signpost that describes an aspect of this protected area's underwater life: the vast meadows of Posidonia oceanica, the starfish; the yellow-striped salema, or "saupe" fish (*Sarpa salpa*); the small, silvery annular seabream, or "sar" (*Diplodus annularis)* with a vertical black stripe at the base of its tail; the Mediterranean rainbow wrasse with young specimens sporting rusty-orange stripes (*Coris Julis*); or the rarer big-headed and pouting dusky grouper, or "mérou brun" (*Epinaphelus marginatus*).

As you snorkel along, a few fish follow you. They are unafraid of people because they remain unharmed by humans in this protected national park.

Symphodus mediterraneus fish,
Photo © M. Barral, PN Port-Cros

Between June 15 and September 15, the park also organizes thirty-minute guided underwater group visits. For more information and reservations, contact the Maison du Parc at Port-Cros during business hours, phone:
+33 (0)4 94 01 40 70.

Note that the park provides no snorkeling or diving equipment. Therefore, either bring your own or check with the local shops at Port-Cros for rentals.

Underwater Panel in Bay of la Palud,
Photo © Ph. Robert, PN Port-Cros

South side, Port-Cros

21 Port-Cros: Sentier des Crêtes

Port-Cros emerges out of the Mediterranean Sea, a slice of the Maures mountain range, with sharp crest-lines and deep ravines.

Along the Vallon de la Solitude Valley that runs from the island's tiny and only village down to its southern tip, green oaks and strawberry trees umbrage a damp footpath that is softened by pine needles and oak leaves.

Further south, through openings in the foliage of Lentisc and green oaks, you peek at the wild coastline below. You might spot a group of Mediterranean shearwaters *(Puffinus yelkouan)* or Cory's shearwaters (*Calonectris diomedea*) clipping the waves. These birds nest in April and May in the relative safety of burrows on the island's sheerest cliffs.

At the summit of Mont Vinaigre (194 meters or 636 feet), you discover a treasure of round mica rocks that glitter in the sun like giant silver coins.

Toward the end of the hike, you reach the only easily accessible beach on the south side of Port-Cros, Plage du Sud. In the summer, many visitors make the half-hour walk from the harbor to dip in Plage du Sud's clear waters or to rest on its powder white sand.

This three-hour hike is longer and more demanding than Port-Cros' Sentier des Plantes loop.

However, it fills you with images of wild cliffs and of paths that burrow through green hills. These visions may well linger indelibly.

View from top of Mont Vinaigre, Port-Cros

View from top of Mont Vinaigre, Port-Cros

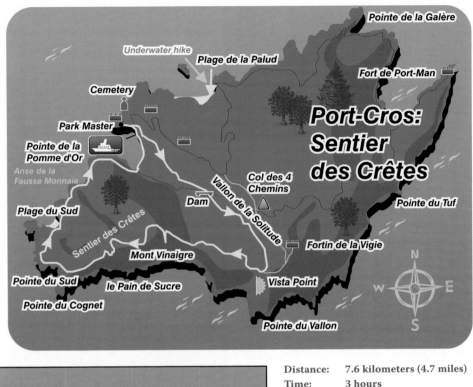

Port-Cros: Sentier des Crêtes

Distance:	7.6 kilometers (4.7 miles)
Time:	3 hours
Elevations:	0–194 meters (0–636 feet)
Difficulty:	Medium
Map:	TOP 25 IGN Map 3446 ET

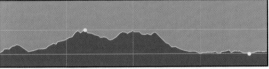

For information on ferryboat access to Port-Cros, see chapter introduction.

Hiking

Begin your hike up the paved path next to the habor's post office. Head up toward the "Plage de la Palud, par la forêt." The little harbor of Port-Cros soon appears behind you.

At the next intersection, head right toward the "Barrage," which a sign describes as fifteen minutes away. You walk by sheets of mica schist rocks, metamorphic rocks that appear foliated, with shiny silver speckles. The Hyères Islands share a common geological past with the Maures Mountains on the continent.

Directions on rock, Port-Cros

At the next intersection, turn right to the *Barrage* (dam) marked on a rock on the side of the path. Continue to follow the path to the "Barrage" and the "Vallon de la Solitude." As you do so, you stroll by a dry stonewall.

At the next intersection, a sign marks the "Col des 4 Chemins." Turn right here and hike by Lentisc or Mastic trees (*Pistacia lentiscus*). You trek past a little house on your left in front of the dam.

At the intersection after the dam, go straight, following the sign to "Les Crêtes 0.20h" and the "Vallon de la Solitude." When you reach the next intersection, go straight to take the "Les Crêtes par la Solitude." You climb steeply for a short while, over roots and rocks, in a damp forest of oaks.

At the top of the hill, turn right toward Mont Vinaigre. A sign tells you the mountain peak is a thirty-minute walk away. The Gabinière Island appears in a window among the thick vegetation of oak and Lentisc. The sides of the little island appear scraped out of the earth. Many boats have sunk in the turbulent waters around the Gabinière.

Gabinière Island, Port-Cros

Further up, you walk by a panel on birds that are spotted around Port-Cros, such as the yellow-legged gull, the black-headed gull, the fast-diving Sandwich tern, and the Yelkouan shearwater. France counts few nesting sites for the pelagic Yelkouan shearwater; a few of these unique nesting sites hide in remote cliffs on Port-Cros.

122

You walk by Aleppo pine trees and large slabs of schist, some horizontal like oval tables, others tilted. At each intersection, follow the trail marked "Mont Vinaigre."

The trail to Mont Vinaigre soon heads steeply up by bushes of thyme, rosemary, and tamarix, a salt-tolerant and salt-secreting shrub. Ten minutes from the intersection, you reach the panoramic top of the mountain.

Return down the same section of path and head left or west toward the Pointe du Cognet. Then follow the signs to the Plage du Sud.

After a tunnel of vegetation, sheared only by the local winds, you turn left to the popular Plage du Sud. This intimate beach boasts white-powder sand with seagulls circling overhead.

You are thirty-five minutes away from your starting point in town. You reach it by continuing on the northeast-bound path by the Pointe de Maitre-Angelin and by the Baie de la Fausse Monnaie and by passing through the southern side of the port.

Plage du Sud, Port-Cros

Pointe du Pin, Porquerolles

22 Porquerolles: East Hike

It's a twenty-minute boat ride from La Tour Fondue on the Giens Peninsula to the island of Porquerolles. Gazing beyond the deck to the crescent-shaped island of Porquerolles, you see only low-lying green hills, slivers of sand like golden ribbons between sea and forest, and a port in the cusp of the island.

The ferryboat arrives in Porquerolles' port by its Lilliputian village. Aside from a string of shops huddled around the square at Place d'Armes and an army of mountain bikes for rent, the village appears untouched by time.

Few motorized vehicles travel the streets of Porquerolles as they require special authorizations. You hear the hum of human voices, the friendly banter of boulistes on the square, kids laughing on their bikes, and in the summer, incessant cicadas.

From the center of town, trails run east, west, and south. On this adventure to the eastern side of Porquerolles, you head for the beach of Notre-Dame that accompanies turquoise waters. You return through the plain of La Courtade by the vineyards of the same name. As you do so, you pass by an intriguing ancient fort-turned-monastery.

124

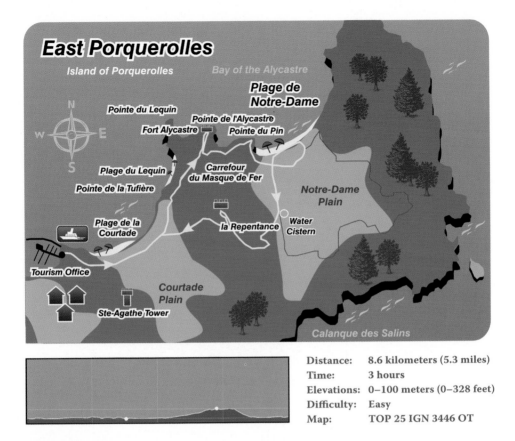

East Porquerolles

Island of Porquerolles · Bay of the Alycastre

Plage de Notre-Dame

Pointe du Lequin
Pointe de l'Alycastre
Fort Alycastre
Pointe du Pin
Plage du Lequin
Carrefour du Masque de Fer
Pointe de la Tufière
Notre-Dame Plain
la Repentance
Water Cistern
Plage de la Courtade
Tourism Office
Courtade Plain
Ste-Agathe Tower
Calanque des Salins

Distance:	8.6 kilometers (5.3 miles)
Time:	3 hours
Elevations:	0–100 meters (0–328 feet)
Difficulty:	Easy
Map:	TOP 25 IGN 3446 OT

For information on ferryboat access to Porquerolles, see chapter introduction.

Hiking:

The hike to the beach of Notre-Dame begins in the village of Porquerolles, on the path by the tourism office marked "Les Plages." It leads to a wide alley bordered by eucalyptus trees.

A sign soon indicates directions for the Conservatoire Botanique National, Fort St. Agathe, Plage d'Argent, Langoustier, Courtade, Oustau de Dieu, and Notre-Dame 2.4 kilometers (1.5 miles) ahead. You take the path for Notre-Dame.

At the Carrefour du Masque de Fer, take a short detour and turn left to visit the ruins of the Fort Alycastre. From the ruins, you peer down the Bay of Alycastre all the way to the northeastern tip of the island, the Cap des Mèdes.

Return to the main path. Pointe du Pin looks over the topaz waters of the Notre-Dame bay.

Plage de Notre Dame, Porquerolles

Just past the Pointe du Pin, you reach the long beach of Notre-Dame and its clear waters. Will you dip in its turquoise waters?

Fort Alycastre, Porquerolles

You return to the village through inland paths; return to the main road through a forest of tree heath, cork oaks, and Aleppo pines. Turn left on the path marked "Calanques des Salins," "Village par l'interieur," "Galère."

After 500 meters (one-third of a mile), at the green water cistern marked PQS8, turn right to "la Repentance" and to the "Village par l'intérieur."

After an uphill hike, a path to the right indicates the way to la Repentance. Once a fort and now an active monastery, la Repentance is not open to the public. We recommend you climb to the Repentance to experience its massive facades and its views that plunge to the sea.

Return to the main path and then turn right, heading east to shoulder the vineyards of the Plaine de la Courtade. These plots of vines produce the wines of Domaine de la Courtade.

The path heads toward the sea and rejoins the main east–west path, which you take on the left (going west) to reach your starting point at the village's port.

Port of Porquerolles

Useful Contacts (for more contacts common to hikes around Hyères, see chapter introduction):

- Domaine de La Courtade Winery: Phone: +33 (0)4 94 58 31 44; E-mail: domaine@lacourtade.com; Web site: www.lacourtade.com
- Domaine Perzinsky Winery: Phone: +33 (0)4 94 58 34 32
- Domaine de l'Ile Winery: Phone: +33 (0) 4 98 04 62 30; Web site: www.domainedelile.com

Above: Plage d'Argent, Porquerolles, in Winter
Below: Plage d'Argent, Porquerolles, in Summer

Aside: Conservatoire Botanique de Porquerolles

On the island of Porquerolles, off the coast of Hyères, fig trees, peach trees, almond trees, and olive trees from France, Italy, and Spain sway in the island breeze as if in a giant nursery.

These trees and many others belong to the *Conservatoire Botanique de Porquerolles* (Porquerolles Botanical Conservatory). Set up on the island of Porquerolles in 1979, the conservatory inventories and preserves plant species, in particular endangered botanical species, Mediterranean species, and ancient species of fruit trees.

In addition to growing these plants on Porquerolles, the conservatory harbors seeds from more than 1,700 species. It also engages in observation and scientific studies that revolve around the impact of climate change. In addition, it opens its door to the public with a permanent exhibition on biodiversity.

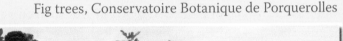

Fig trees, Conservatoire Botanique de Porquerolles

Useful Contacts:

- Conservatoire Botanique de Porquerolles: E–mail: cbnmp@cbnmed.org; Web site: www.portcrosparcnational.fr/conservatoire

129

Northwestern coast of Porquerolles

23 Porquerolles: West Hike

Heading west on the bicycle-friendly island of Porquerolles, you visit the white-as-talc beach of Plage d'Argent, curved between a natural pier of brown shale and a forest of pine trees. Beach lovers appreciate this spot for its sand, for its half-hour walking distance from the island's town, and for its summertime beach-side snack shop and restaurant.

You continue to the western tip of the island, by the secluded Mas du Langoustier Hotel and its delectable restaurant, L'Olivier. This fancy complex is owned by the Fournier family, descendants of François Joseph Fournier. Mr. Fournier bought the island of Porquerolles in 1912, after learning of its auctioned sale, and offered it as a wedding present to his newly wedded wife Sylvia.

You continue to the Langoustier Peninsula where, under France's King Louis XIV in the mid-seventeenth century, Cardinal Richelieu ordered the construction of the Fort du Langoustier. From the fort's ruins, you spot the island of the Petit Langoustier and its fort, the Giens Peninsula. Further out, you spy the bay of Toulon. You return to the village through a forest and back to the coastal path.

Enjoy the family-friendly hike year round, but bring plenty of water as supplies are limited outside of town.

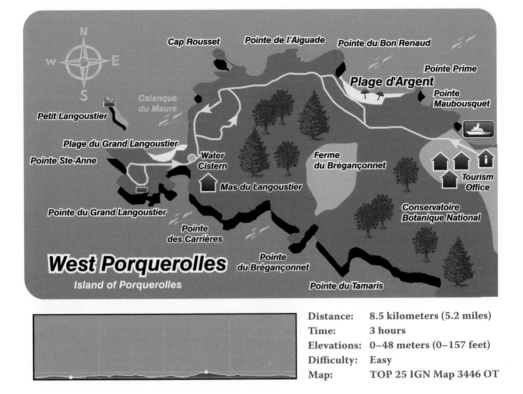

West Porquerolles

Island of Porquerolles

Distance:	8.5 kilometers (5.2 miles)
Time:	3 hours
Elevations:	0–48 meters (0–157 feet)
Difficulty:	Easy
Map:	TOP 25 IGN Map 3446 OT

For information on ferryboat access to Porquerolles, see chapter introduction.

Hiking:

From the main square, the Place d'Armes, continue west on Rue de la Ferme and turn right on the Chemin du Langoustier. You pass by the vineyards of the Domaine Perzinsky, one of the island's three wine producers (Domaine Perzinsky, Domaine de l'Ile, and Domaine de la Courtade). Rows of eucalyptus trees and mimosas accompany you.

At a Y-intersection in the road, a sign indicates that Plage d'Argent lies 0.3 kilometer away. You follow the sign and stroll along the wide path, heading slightly downhill. You soon pass a sign that points toward "Calanque de Brégançonnet" and "Langoustier par les Crêtes," and continue on the main path.

At the next Y in the road, you turn right where a sign indicates "Plage d'Argent, (still) 0.3 kilometer" away.

As usual on bike-loving Porquerolles, low fences of wooden logs allow visitors to park and secure their bicycles before heading to the beach. You kick off your hiking shoes to feel the powder-like fine white-quartz sand of Plage d'Argent.

Continue on the beach of Plage d'Argent, by its snack bar, past its beach guard post, and across sea-lapped rocks to the Anse du Bon Renaud.

Head inland through a small forest of oak trees and strawberry trees (*Arbutus unedo*),

Plage d'Argent, Porquerolles

and turn right on the path that indicates "Pointe de l'Aiguade."

Return to the main path and turn right (west) toward the Langoustier, now 1.3 kilometers ahead. At the PQS2 water cistern, go straight toward the Plage du Grand Langoustier.

You might want to stop by the Calanque du Maure and see the Ile du Petit Langoustier islet with the ruins of its round tower. The vegetation around the Calanque du Maure hugs the ground, sculpted by the wind.

Head back to the main path to the Langoustier, which is now 0.5 kilometer ahead. Pass by the four-star hotel Le Mas du Langoustier. Note that if you fancy a delectable meal, the L'Olivier restaurant serves wonderful dishes. At the Y-intersection by the PQS1 cistern, turn left to the "Langoustier."

Pointe Ste.Anne, Porquerolles

Pass the bike park, enter the chained road—where bikes are not allowed to circle around Pointe Ste. Anne and Pointe du Grand-Langoustier—and enjoy the panoramic views of the Ile du Langoustier, Ile du Grand Ribaud, Giens Peninsula, and the northwestern side of Porquerolles.

Return through the same path to the sign with Pointe des Carrières, Brégançonnet, Village par l'Interieur. Turn right here to head inland up roots and rocks into a deep forest.

At the intersection with the main path, turn left to follow the road "Village par Bord de Mer."

At the PQS2 cistern, turn right. The path takes you behind Plage d'Argent. By the vineyards, turn left and return to the Place d'Armes in the village.

Pointe Prime, Porquerolles

Useful Contacts (for more contacts common to hikes around Hyères, see chapter introduction):

- Plage d'Argent Restaurant; open from April to end of September; Phone: +33 (0)4 94 58 32 48
- Le Mas du Langoustier, four–star hotel and restaurant: Phone: +33 (0)4 94 58 30 09; Web site: www.langoustier.com
- Domaine de La Courtade Winery: Phone: +33 (0)4 94 58 31 44; E–mail: domaine@lacourtade.com; Web site: www.lacourtade.com
- Domaine Perzinsky Winery: Phone: +33 (0)4 94 58 34 32
- Domaine de l'Ile Winery: Phone: +33 (0) 4 98 04 62 30; Web site: www.domainedelile.com
- Conservatoire Botanique de Porquerolles: E–mail: cbnmp@cbnmed.org; Web site: www.portcrosparcnational.fr/conservatoire

View of Ile Longue, West side of the Giens Peninsula

24 Giens Peninsula, West Side

Within reach of the town of Hyères, a double isthmus of sand reaches south four kilometers (2.5 miles) into the sea and holds, at its tip, the Giens Peninsula. Between its two fragile fingers of sand that poke into the sea, the Giens Peninsula harbors the salt marshes of Les Salins des Pesquiers and the Etangs des Pesquiers, where migratory birds such as pink flamingos, egrets, and herons come visit.

From atop the small town of Giens, where Nobel Prize poet St. John Perse is buried, the Golden Isles of Porquerolles, Port-Cros, and le Levant stretch like ribbons across the sea. Some 18,000 years ago, when the Mediterranean Sea was 125 meters (410 feet) below its current levels, you could have walked from the Giens Peninsula to the Golden Islands of Hyères.

Today, we invite you to walk on the western side of the Giens Peninsula, along the coastal path. After the quiet port of La Madrague, you discover a coastline where cliffs plunge precipitously into the sea and dark rocks display their geologic torments through folds and twirls.

The peninsula's summit at Escampobariou brandishes its peak at 116 meters (380 feet) over the sea. Your climb around it on slabs of rocks and roots adds grandeur to an already gorgeous and energetic hike.

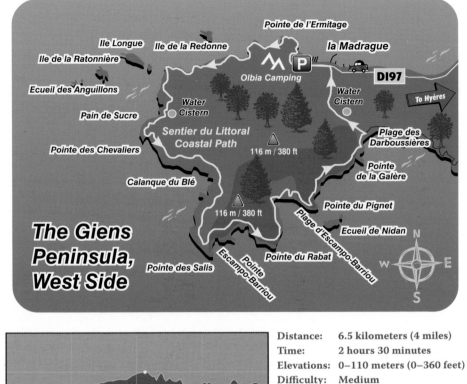

The Giens Peninsula, West Side

Distance:	6.5 kilometers (4 miles)
Time:	2 hours 30 minutes
Elevations:	0–110 meters (0–360 feet)
Difficulty:	Medium
Map:	TOP 25 IGN Map 3446 OT

Getting there:

From the Hyères port, take the Route de la Capte/D97. Pass La Capte and turn right at the roundabout that indicates La Madrague. After the port of La Madrague, park on a sandy lot on the left side of the street, before the "Camping Olbia" campground.

Hiking:

Reach the beach through a path marked "accès à la mer" among a field of reeds. Note that there are few beaches on the western tip of the Giens Peninsula.

From here all the way to the Plage des Darboussières beach on the south-western side of the peninsula, you hike on the *Sentier du Littoral* (Coastal Path) marked in yellow paint marks. Stay on the trail closest to the coast and you can't get lost.

135

You notice an islet out to sea and continue up to the Pointe de l'Ermitage among a protected site of Aleppo pine trees. The path alternates between bushy passages among maquis vegetation of green oaks, tamarix trees or salt cedars, and climbing sarsaparilla, and open salt-whipped creeks and coves.

At the top of a promontory, a cement bunker overlooks the islands of Ile Longue, Ile de la Ratonnière, and, further out, Iles des Fourmiques. You head down by a protected area that is delimited for conservation and re-habilitation.

Pass the HRS08 green water cistern and notice the menhir-looking rock of the Pain de Sucre sticking out of the sea. At the Pointe des Chevaliers, rocks of schist display their deep brown layers.

You keep to the right path, the one closest to the sea, and penetrate a thick oak forest where you hear the distant sound of crashing waves. You briefly emerge out of the forest at the Calanque du Blé then climb steeply around the Pointe des Salis, traversing over rocks that are stratified like petrified wood.

You head down a forested path over sand, rocks, roots, and pine needles with regular window openings to the sea. A steep downhill takes you around the Pointe du Rabat. At each intersection, continue taking the seaside path.

West side of the Giens Peninsula

You reach the cute beach of Pontillon with charcoal-colored rocks at its sides. You continue around the Pointe du Pignet and through a steep downhill to the Pointe de la Galère. You reach the Darboussières beach with its sprinkling of houses.

Turn inland at the Darboussières beach to reach a water cistern. Take the path on the left closest to the cistern.

At the end of the path (cross a green metallic barrier), take the small paved road on the right that presents a sea view of the Rade de Giens. At the street intersection, turn left on the Avenue René de Knyff D197 road for a ten-minute walk to your starting point.

Useful Contacts:

- Les Amis de la Presqu'île de Giens: Supporters of the Giens Peninsula's natural sites. Organizes botanical and geological outings (in French): Phone: +33(0)4 94 58 20 65; Web site: www.apgiens.com
- Hyères Tourist Information Office: E-mail: info@ot-hyeres.fr; Phone: +33(0)4 94 01 84 50; Web site: www.hyeres-tourisme.com
- Maison du Tourisme de la Provence d'Azur: For information and reservations on a wide variety of local activities. E-mail: contact@amusezvous.fr; Phone: +33(0)4 94 38 50 91; Web site: www.amusezvous.fr

From the top of Mont Fenouillet

25 Mont Fenouillet

Like an island of trees tucked between the urban sites of Toulon and Hyères, the mountain of Mont Fenouillet offers a forested enclave that is much appreciated by nature lovers. The *adret* (southern) side of the hill is covered in densely growing shrubs, while the damper *ubac* (northern) flank harbors a variety of heathers, moss, and older cork oak trees, where insects thrive.

Mont Fenouillet sits at a cross-point between the chalky-white limestone chains of Provence to the west around Toulon (Faron, Gros-Cerveau, Croupatier, Coudon, and Mont Caume) and the much older crystalline mountain range of the Maures to the east (Colle-Noire, Maurettes, and Maures). You can see much of this surrounding geography from the summit of Mont Fenouillet.

Graptolite fossils discovered in the schist rocks on Fenouillet helped to date the Fenouillet's Silurien rocks to about 440 million years of age. You may spot a few rock-climbers dangling on great blocks of quartzite by the thirteenth-century chapel on top of the hill.

Most of the area around Mont Fenouillet is privately owned, though hiking is tolerated along its paths. As always, neither leave anything behind nor take anything away.

138

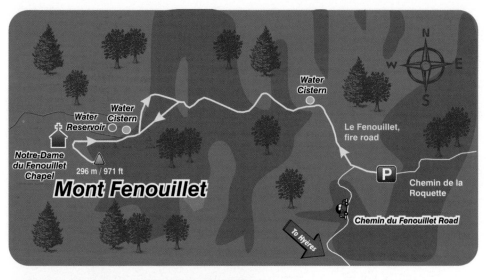

Distance:	4 kilometer (2.5 miles)
Time:	1 hour 15 minutes
Elevations:	157–281 meters (515–922 feet)
Difficulty:	Easy
Map:	TOP 25 IGN Map 3446 OT

Getting there:

From the N98 road at Hyères, at the main roundabout called Henri Petit, turn onto the Alexis Godillot road heading toward La Crau and La Bayorre. At end of Alexis Godillot, turn left onto the Avenue de Toulon. Just before the pastry shop "Le Moulin de la Poterie," turn right onto the Chemin du Fenouillet road. Note that the pastry shop sells bread and sandwiches to bring along for a picnic (phone: +33 (0)4 94 65 71 00). Go up the Chemin du Fenouillet by villas until you reach a T in the road. At the T, the fire road "Le Fenouillet" begins on your left. Turn right onto Chemin de la Roquette and park on the side of the street away from traffic.

Hiking:

Walk back to the fire road "Le Fenouillet" and veer right onto this paved path. On your left, the Mont Fenouillet appears in the distance with a cross and antenna at its summit. Continue on the Le Fenouillet paved road, passing the "La Roquette" fire path on your right, a water cistern marked HRS02, and the "Le Barrage" path on your left. On your

Mont Fenouillet

left and below, traffic hums. On your right, a quilt of cultivated parcels lies quiet. To the south, the island of Porquerolles comes into view as the road climbs.

You reach an intersection with a majestic old cork oak tree at its center and the HRS03 water cistern ahead. Head left toward the green gate that leads to the Chapel of Notre Dame du Fenouillet. Enter through the side of the gate. Behind the restored chapel, you will find a small path covered in vegetation. The path heads up to the top of Mont Fenouillet. It is fairly steep and requires a bit of climbing over rocks, so be very careful if you decide to go all the way

From the top of Mont Fenouillet

140

up. Return to the small chapel using the same small path, and then to the intersection point with the tall cork oak tree.

When facing the green HRS03 cistern, take the first dirt path that goes up into an oak forest. Navigate between large boulders on a path marked with red paint dots. As the path heads down, you discover a platform of wood and metal behind rocks and bushes. The platform opens to a 360-degree view.

Continue down into the damp, thick forest. At a four-way intersection of paths, turn right. You notice a one-way road sign pinned on a tall oak tree. Turn right here.

The path leads back to the "Le Fenouillet" paved road. Veer left on it and pass the HRS02 cistern. Follow the "La Roquette" path until you reach the street where you parked.

Useful Contacts:

- Hyères Tourist Information Office: E—mail: info@ot—hyeres.fr; Phone: +33(0) 4 94 01 84 50; Web site: www.hyeres—tourisme.com
- Maison du Tourisme de la Provence d'Azur: For information and reservations on a wide variety of local activities. E—mail: contact@amusezvous.fr; Phone: +33(0)4 94 38 50 91; Web site: www.amusezvous.fr

Dolmen de Gaoutabry

26 Dolmen of Gaoutabry

If you have seen monumental Stonehenge or the large prehistoric standing stones that point to the sky in Brittany, the Dolmen of Gaoutabry, with its lineup of thin, upright stone slabs, may appear modest.

However, this prehistoric burial site dates back to the early Copper Age some 4,500 years ago, and with its six meters of length and 1.5 meters of width (19.6 by 3.2 feet), it represents the largest dolmen currently known in the Var Department of France. Discovered in 1876 by the Baron de Bonstetten, it was classified as an historic monument in 1988.

Standing atop a hill four kilometers (2.5 miles) north of the village of La Lon-de-les-Maures, the megaliths of local mica schist rocks form a rectangle that lies east–west. In a row, this rectangular stone-cropping includes a burial chamber, an antechamber, and an entrance that opens up exactly due west.

To some, the dolmen's orientation and its extended chamber speak of a symbolic "inverted birth." Incinerated remains of the dead were brought in through the hall and its two "legs," through the antechamber or "belly," and up to rest in the site's burial chamber or "head." The Dolmen of Gaoutabry still harbors many mysteries. Its archaeologists have found the cremated remains of thirty-

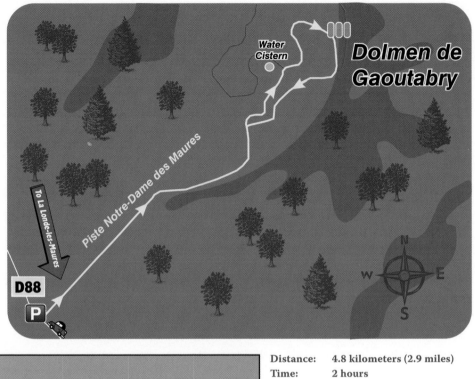

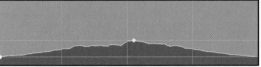

Distance:	4.8 kilometers (2.9 miles)
Time:	2 hours
Elevations:	43–196 meters (141–643 feet)
Difficulty:	Easy
Map:	TOP 25 IGN Map 3446 OT

four individuals along with a number of arrows and blades, many of which are on display today at the Archaeological Museum of St. Raphaël.

The dolmen sits on private property with access by pedestrians and bikers tolerated. To reach the dolmen, you hike above rolling hills covered with the region's famous vineyards. Because much of the trail is exposed to the sun, we recommend you hike it outside of hot summer days.

Getting there:

Take the N98 road to La Londe-les-Maures and head north on the D88 towards Collobrières. Pass the Château de Jasson winery. After about 2.1 kilometers (1.3 miles) from La Londe-les-Maures, you reach the Ginouvier residential area and the "Piste Notre-Dame des Maures" path on the right. Cars are not allowed on this fire road. Park by the trailhead, away from traffic and clear of the trail's entrance.

Head up the "Piste Notre-Dame des Maures" rocky trail, continuing straight on the main trail. Pass by the B51 Notre Dame des Maures road barrier and sign.

After 2.2 kilometers (1.3 miles) of gentle climbing, you reach an intersection with a green water cistern marked LMS12.

Sign for the Dolmen de Gaoutabry

Take the small footpath that heads up, to the left of the green LMS12 cistern.

Turn right at the next path that heads up. Signs for the dolmen accompany you along the way. Walk up a few steps to reach the dolmen on the hill's panoramic summit at 198 meters (650 feet).

Return through the same rocky path by bushes of thorny brooms, by the upswept branches of tree heaths, and by cork oak trees. Notice the vineyards below, by the D88. Vineyards cover more than half of the land around the district of La Londe-les-Maures, and they produce fine "Côte de Provence" wines.

Useful Contacts:

- La Londe–les–Maures Tourist Information Office: Phone: +33 (0)4 94 01 53 10; E–mail: lalonde.tourisme@wanadoo.fr; Web site: www.ot–lalondelesmaures.fr

Aside: Salins de Pesquiers

Between the two arms of sand that form the Giens Peninsula's tombolo by the city of Hyères, as many of 600 pink flamingos (*Phoenicopterus roseus*) stroll across the shallow waters of the Pesquiers wetlands. Groups of them poke their heads under water, their long necks dangling like noodles over the pond. The birds stamp the mud with their webbed feet and stir the thick, brown, soupy waters. With their bills, they filter the water to feed on seeds, larvae, algae, and little fish. Behind the flamingos, above a drape of low-lying reeds, a tiny Zitting Cisticola bird (*Cisticola juncidis*) tweets.

The birds evolve in a patchwork of rectangular ponds. Along the side of the ponds, old pumps and levees hint of the area's past. From 1858 until 1995, most of the 600 hectares (1,482 acres) of the Salins des Pesquiers worked as saltpans. Sun and wind dried up the shallow saltpans, leaving crusts of salt that were extracted and sold.

After salt mining at Pesquiers stopped for economic reasons, the Conservatoire du Littoral acquired the wetlands in 2001 for land and wildlife protection. Today, on a guided visit of the wetlands, you might observe pink flamingos, black-winged stilts, red-billed common shelducks, gray herons, egrets, or any of the 200 different species of birds that have been spotted here.

Note that to keep the site as wild and undisturbed as possible, only guided visits are allowed at the Salins des Pesquiers. Contact the *League pour la Protection des Oiseaux* (LPO), or League for the Protection of Birds, that organizes bird-watching visits by phone: +33 (0)4 94 12 79 52, or the Maison du Tourisme by phone: +33(0)4 94 38 50 91.

Appendix A: Local Sports Stores

- L'Aventure, Sanary-sur-Mer: Specialized sports shop for hiking, mountain trekking, and rock-climbing; 194 ancien chemin de Toulon, Sanary-sur-Mer; Phone: +33 (0)4 98 00 03 40; Web site: www.laventure.fr

- Azur Tri and Run: Specialized sports shop for running, biking, swimming, and triathlons; La Palud, Impasse Thomas Edison, Fréjus; Phone : +33 (0)4 94 54 69 64; Web site: www.azurtriandrun.com

- Decathlon: Sporting goods chain store; corporate Web site: www.decathlon.fr; Stores in the Var:

  - Decathlon Fréjus: Zone d'activités, La Palud 2 Lotissement de l'intendance, Fréjus; Phone: +33 (0)4 98 12 71 71

  - Decathlon La Garde: Zone d'activités commerciales, Grand Ciel, La Garde; Phone: +33 (0)4 94 14 79 50

  - Decathlon Ollioules: Quartier QUIEZ, Centre commercial Carrefour, Ollioules; Phone : +33 (0)4 94 18 95 40

  - Decathlon Trans en Provence: Quartier Saint Roch, Route Nationale 555, Trans en Provence; Phone: +33 (0)4 94 50 96 96

- GO Sport: Sporting goods chain store; corporate Web site: www.go-sport.com; Stores in the Var:

  - GO Sport, Toulon, Centre Commercial Grand Var, La Valette du Var; Phone: +33 (0)4 94 14 09 09

  - GO Sport, Toulon, Mayol, Centre Commercial Mayol, Toulon; Phone: +33 (0)4 98 00 97 30

  - GO Sport, Fréjus, Quartier de la Tuilière, RN7, Puget-sur-Argens/Fréjus; Phone: +33 (0)4 98 11 14 90

- InterSport: Sporting goods chain store; corporate Web site: www.intersport.fr; Stores in the Var:

  - InterSport Brignoles: Centre Commercial Leclerc, Brignoles; Phone: +33 (0)4 98 05 02 66

  - InterSport St. Raphaël: 61 Ave. Victor Hugo, St. Raphaël; Phone: +33 (0)4 94 95 81 54

  - Sport Leader Fréjus: RN7, Fréjus; Phone: +33 (0)4 94 40 93 84

  - InterSport Le Lavandou: Parc la Méridienne, Le Lavandou; Phone: +33 (0)4 94 64 92 52

- Sport 2000: Sporting goods chain store; corporate Web site: www.sport2000.fr; Stores in the Var:

  - Sport 2000, Cogolin, Rue Marceau: Phone: +33 (0)4 94 56 29 21

  - Sport 2000, Hyères, Centre Olbia: Phone: +33 (0)4 94 48 01 68

  - Sport 2000, Ste. Maxime, Centre Commercial Hyper Champion: Phone: +33 (0)4 94 96 27 28

Appendix B: Useful Contacts

Paramedics (SAMU): 15
Fire: 18
Police: 17

To call France from another country, dial 33 for France's country code, then the French nine-digit phone number without the leading zero.

To call within France, dial the ten-digit phone number that includes a leading zero. In the southeastern region of France, fixed phone lines begin with the numbers 04, while most cell phone numbers begin with the numbers 06.

TOURIST INFORMATION OFFICES:

- Agay Tourist Information Office: Phone: +33(0)4 94 82 01 85; E-mail: info@agay.fr; Web site: www.agay.fr

- Bagnols-en-Forêt Tourist Information Office: Phone: +33(0)4 94 40 64 68; E-mail: bagnols-en-foret.tourisme@wanadoo.fr; Web site: http://www.ot-bagnols.com/

- Bormes-les-Mimosas Tourist Information Office: Phone: +33 (0)4 94 01 38 38; E-mail: mail@bormeslesmimosas.com; Web site: www.bormeslesmimosas.com

- Collobrières Tourist Office: Phone: +33 (0)4 94 48 08 00; E-mail: contact@collobrieres-tourisme.com; Web site: www.collobrieres-tourisme.com

- Fréjus Tourist Information Office: Phone: + 33 (0)4 94 51 83 83; E-mail: tourisme@frejus.fr; Web site: www.frejus.fr

- Hyères Tourist Information Office: Phone: +33(0)4 94 01 84 50; E-mail: info@ot-hyeres.fr; Web site: www.ot-hyeres.fr/en/

- La Croix Valmer Tourist Office: Phone: +33 (0)4 94 55 12 12; Web site: lacroixvalmer.fr/

- La Garde-Freinet Tourist Office: Phone: +33 (0)4 94 43 67 41; E-mail: info@lagardefreinet.com; Web site: www.lagardefreinet-tourisme.com

- Le Lavandou Tourist Office: Phone: +33 (0)4 94 00 40 50; E-mail: info@ot-lelavandou.fr; Web site: www.ot-lelavandou.fr

- La Londe-les-Maures Tourist Information Office: Phone: +33 (0)4 94 01 53 10; E-mail: lalonde.tourisme@wanadoo.fr; Web site: www.ot-lalondelesmaures.fr

- Ramatuelle Tourist Information Office: Phone: +33 (0)4 98 12 64 00; Web site: www.ramatuelle-tourisme.com/

- Roquebrune-sur-Argens Tourist Information Office: Phone: +33 (0)4 94 19 89 89; E-mail: tourisme@roquebrunesurargens.fr; Web Site: www.roquebrune.com/

- Ste. Maxime Tourist Information Office: Phone: +33 (0)4 94 55 75 55;
  Web site: www.ste-maxime.com/

- St. Raphaël Tourist Information Office: Phone: +33(0)4 94 19 52 52;
  E-mail: information@saint-raphael.com; Web site: www.saint-raphael.com

- St. Tropez Tourist Information Office: Phone: 0892 68 48 28 (calling charges may apply);
  Web site: www.ot-saint-tropez.com/

- Maison du Tourisme du Golfe de St. Tropez, booking center for the region around
  St. Tropez: Phone: +33 (0)4 94 55 22 00; E-mail: info@st-tropez-lesmaures.com;
  Web site: www.st-tropez-lesmaures.com

- Maison du Tourisme de la Provence d'Azur, booking center for the region around Hyères,
  including ferryboat access and hotel reservations for the Golden Islands and Hyères.
  Phone: +33 (0)4 94 38 50 91; E-mail: contact@amusezvous.fr; Web site: www.amusezvous.fr

- France Guide, the official Web site of the French Government Tourist Office:
  uk.franceguide.com

TRANSPORTS

For local bus services:

- Société Départementale de Transports du Var (SODETAV): Phone: +33 (0)4 94 12 55 12;
  Web site: www.sodetrav.fr/lignesinterurbaines.htm

Ferryboat companies:

For ferryboat access to the Hyères Islands:

- TLV Transports Littoral Varois: Phone: +33 (0)4 94 58 21 8;1 E-mail: infos@tlv-tvm.com;
  Web site: www.tlv-tvm.com, for access from Hyères and the Giens Peninsula

- Vedettes des Iles d'Or: Web site: www.vedettesilesdor.fr, for access from La Croix-Valmer,
  Le Lavandou, Cavalaire, and La Londe-les-Maures

For ferryboat access within the St. Tropez Bay (e.g., from Ste. Maxime to St. Tropez):

- Les Bateaux Verts: Phone: +33 (0) 4 94 49 29 39; Web site: www.bateauxverts.com

French railway company SNCF: Web site: www.sncf.com, includes information in English

SITES AND ASSOCIATIONS

- Conservatoire Botanique de Porquerolles: E-mail: cbnmp@cbnmed.org;
  Web site: www.portcrosparcnational.fr/conservatoire

- Conservatoire du Littoral: Web site: www.conservatoire-du-littoral.fr

- Espaces Naturels de Provence: Phone : +33 (0)4 42 20 03 83; Web site: www.ceep.asso.fr

148

- Fédération Française de la Randonnée Pédestre (French Rambling/Hiking Association): Web site: www.ffrandonnee.fr in English and German: www.ffrandonnee.eu
- La Verne Monastery: Phone: +33 (0)4 94 43 48 28
- Les Amis de la Presqu'île de Giens: Supporters of the Giens Peninsula's natural sites. Organizes botanical and geological outings (in French). Phone: +33(0)4 94 58 20 65; Web site: www.apgiens.com
- Parc National de Port-Cros: E-mail: accueil.pnpc@espaces-naturels.fr; Web site: www.portcrosparcnational.fr

WEATHER

- Météo France Weather Forecast: Web site: www.meteofrance.com

STAY IN TOUCH

We would love to hear about your trip on the Côte d'Azur and your hikes.

To share your hiking experience, ask questions, or find out the latest on new and existing hiking paths across the Côte d'Azur, come visit our Web site: www.azuralive.com.

From the azuralive.com Web site, find out how to order this book online. Ask about quantity discounts available on bulk purchases of this book for your fundraisers, for promotional programs, or as gifts to your friends or customers.

Index